# Alpha Male Strategies

*Teaching guys dating strategies in the social media age*

## Social Media Dating Age

As most men know, it's harder than ever to date in today's world. With dating apps, Facebook, Instagram, etc., women have more options than ever. Women are more selective than ever with so many options at their fingertips. They're screening harder and harder for confident, high-value men. In today's social media age, a non-confident man is a sex-deprived man.

When I was in my late teens and early twenties, I don't remember women flaking on dates. Maybe they did with other guys, but they didn't flake on me. I don't know if it was my six-foot-four muscular frame or my pretty boy looks but women didn't flake on me. In today's world, even I get flaked on. I've had women flake on me an hour before the date with little to no notice. Dealing with this kind of flakiness from women, any rational male is obviously going to come up with strategies to combat it.

First, let's talk about why women want a high-value man. A high-value man is a man in demand. He's a man whose free time is valuable because he doesn't have much free time. He's a man who's primarily concerned with pursuing his purpose. A high-value man is a man who's too busy to be needy. Women naturally gravitate to him because he's a challenge. Guys who are not focused on their purpose are men whose free time is abundant and therefore they are not a challenge. This availability naturally turns women off. This signals to women that other women obviously aren't occupying his time. Women gain attraction when they know other women want you. How many times have you been single and no woman would give you the time of day but the second you got a girlfriend, every woman was looking your way? That's because the woman you're with has raised your sexual market value. I don't know if it's biology or what, but let's face it; women hate men who are too available. If you're a man reading this and you want to attract hotter women, the first thing you might consider is to start getting focused on your purpose.

## FEMINISM

There might not be a bigger culprit in the dating world than feminism. Feminism has changed women and not for the better, either. Feminism has taught women to let men do all the pursuing. Women are taught that since they have the vagina a man should do 100% of the pursuing. Now, I know a lot of blue pilled men are going to say "Hey, isn't a man supposed to do all the pursuing in the beginning?" Unfortunately, men are being taught this feminized western society way of thinking. Men, you have value also, just because you don't have a vagina doesn't mean you shouldn't be pursued also. Both men and women want to feel wanted. Women show this disinterest to gain the "power" in the relationship. The power in the relationship is basically who has the upper hand. Whoever has the upper hand controls the relationship. Feminists believe women should control men. The best way to get men in the submissive position is to have men do all the pursuing. Pursuing is being submissive in a lot of ways. Women are taught that men should do all the pursuing and if he doesn't want to pursue, oh well, he must didn't have high enough interest. So as men we have to play the "game" in the beginning. That means we have no other choice but to do all the pursuing in the beginning, but here's the rub. Once women develop feelings you can slowly back away until they're doing all the pursuing. It's easy for women to apply the feminist agenda when they care nothing about you but once you've gotten her to a place where she's catching feelings, all that feminism crap goes right out the window. There's a secret to getting women to chase or pursue you. When you call women consistently for dates they have the assurance that you'll call for a date so there's no need to pursue you. You have to take that comfort away. you need to become a little more erratic in your behavior. So instead of being predictable and calling to set up a date every week which leads to a flake eventually anyway because the more unpredictable guy calls out the blue and takes your date away. You call her so you don't come across as a heartless prick but skip weeks asking her out until she says those 6 magic words: "Am I seeing you this weekend?" Congratulations, she's officially pursuing you. Now don't go get comfortable yet. The game never ends. The biggest reason guys lose their girlfriends is because they get too comfortable and by comfortable I mean they let their girls have the comfort of knowing exactly where they stand. You got to always let a woman feel as if she's more interested in you than you are in her. Once a woman feels you're more into her than she is into you her attraction could drop drastically.

## BLUE PILL

Most men fall into this category. These men have absolutely no understanding of female nature. The blue and red pill reference comes from the movie The Matrix. Basically, men who digested the red pill see the world for the way it truly is. Which means they have a true understanding of female nature. This simply means they understand that women are incapable of truly loving a man. Now of course there are unicorns but don't live your life hoping to find a unicorn just like you wouldn't live your life hoping to hit the lottery. Blue pill men are unaware of this and are usually blindsided when they fall on extended hard times and the woman bails. This is important to know because as long as I've been living at some point no matter who you are, hard times will hit. No one is above life's trials and tribulations. This doesn't mean you'll be homeless but what it does mean is that maybe those expensive getaways you and your significant other would take twice a year maybe you can't afford to do them a couple years. Blue pill men tend not to be jealous because they're completely unaware of female nature. There's a theory that women prefer to sleep with alpha males when they're ovulating. In other words, women want to reproduce with an alpha male. I can tell you from friends of mine finding out the child or children weren't theirs after getting a paternity test. It usually takes a man to go through something personally or a close friend or relative before they fully digest the red pill. Until they have a real life revelation they'll probably classify you as bitter so it really does no good to try to convince them otherwise.

## PURPLE PILL

Men who are purple pill have a full understanding of female nature and have decided to just accept it. These men have a tendency to be jealous because they have a full understanding that women will step out and pursue the alpha male if given the chance. Most alpha males will more than likely enter or re-enter this stage at some point later in life when they're tired of sleeping around and seek companionship. Don't get me wrong, they are still more than likely going to step out from time to time but at this stage in their life they're looking for more and so they just accept female nature for what it is and sleep with one eye open.

## RED PILL

Red pill men not only have a full understanding of female nature but also choose to not enter into anything monogamous because of it. Being red pill doesn't mean you're an alpha male or ladies' man. In fact, most men who are red pill are beta males who discovered female nature the hard way. Red pill men have a tendency to come off bitter but they're typically not bitter at women but they're bitter at the fact that they understand they have two choices to choose from. They can either go through life continuing to just date and never start a family or have anything meaningful or they can just accept female nature for what it is and move on. That reality can cause most men to come off as bitter. It's not that they're bitter, it's just that they deep down know eventually they'll probably want to have something meaningful and the simple fact that women are truly incapable of loving them back is quite depressing.

## MASTER THE ABILITY TO BE ALONE

Before the self-improvement and before any strategy or technique there's one thing every man must master before he's able to be a chick magnet. That's the ability to be alone. Resources come and go, looks fade and so it's natural for most men's confidence to wane from time to time depending on what the weight scale or his bank statement says. So if you're dating a woman and you're a little unsure of yourself due to your business going through a little downturn, how are you supposed to stand up to her? The answer is, you don't mind being alone. When you have no fear of going out by yourself, spending a Friday or Saturday night home alone or at a bar by yourself, you my friend can handle any woman's confidence test or commonly known as shit test. Being on your mission and purpose in life helps with this aspect because when you have a purpose you're never really alone. Your purpose starts to take over your life and you start to look at women or anybody for that matter as a distraction. Mastering the ability to be alone goes deeper than just standing up to women. It also helps you disassociate with family members and friends who are not supportive or just negative in general. A lot of them tolerate bad, negative behavior from so-called friends and family members who never have anything positive to say. You should be surrounding yourself with positive people who have positive things to say and pushing you to new heights.

## SELF IMPROVEMENT

Now I know a lot of guys try to avoid this area because it requires hard work. Most guys when they set out to attract women they instantly gravitate towards GAME. Guys game is important and I'm not here to try and convince you otherwise but the fact of the matter is self-improvement is just as important, if not more. Fellas you can improve your GAME and strategy all you want but if you don't improve your finances and physique you'll probably never attract the QUALITY of woman you want. When I say attract, I simply mean you have to get your foot in the door to apply some strategies. Most women won't even take a man serious if his finances aren't in order or she finds him sexually attractive.

Guys let's face it, women are attracted to successful men. You might not like it but we all know it's true. While getting women is a good byproduct of wanting to achieve success, every man should want to be successful for himself. The fact of the matter is women like men with resources because she knows he would be able to provide if she chooses to bear kids with him. It doesn't mean you have to have kids with her but you can enjoy a lot of sex while she decides.

Of course you have your gold diggers who only want a man's resources but most women don't want a man of resources for shopping sprees, most want a man with resources for simple provision.

Now that you're well on your way to financial success lets discuss body improvements. Women love a well-defined body. They settle for the dad bod if the man displays beta male provider qualities, but all things equal she would definitely prefer the nicer physique. Hey guys, let me dispel the myth women don't care about the physical. They care! Maybe not as much as men but they care. Now guys I'm not saying you need to be as ripped as Brat Pitt in Fight Club but you need to try to get into the best shape you possibly can to attract the highest quality mate you can. I've been overweight in my life and let me tell you the way women have sex with you when they find you sexually appealing and the way they have sex with you when it's more of a personality connection is two different things.

## Game

Now that we've got the self-improvement out the way lets discuss your game. What is game? Game simply is the strategy you use to create or maintain attraction. If a woman doesn't find you at least somewhat attractive no amount of game will help you. You have to be at least a 5 on a scale of 1-10 to have a shot to raise it. You have to raise her attraction level to at least a 7 to have sex with her and at least a 9 before you hear those 3 magic words: "I Love You." Now the strategy I use to raise a woman's attraction level is displaying I'm a HIGH-VALUE MALE.

Before we go any further let's define HIGH-VALUE MALE. A high-value male is simply a man who is primarily focused on his passion and purpose in life. He lives a life of social abundance and moves to the beat of his own drum. He doesn't have time to chase women, he's too busy pursuing his goals and dreams. He pursues a woman in the beginning but if he gets any resistance he has an abundance mindset and simply moves on. To become a high-value man you must first find out what your purpose is. Your purpose has to be something you love to do and are passionate about. It can't just be something you make a lot of money doing. When you're passionate about something you're naturally going to work longer and harder at because you enjoy doing it. Ever wonder why some athletes and entertainers get so good at their craft while others remain the same or even worse, regress? That's because the entertainers and athletes who really enjoyed their craft put more time into honing their craft than the entertainers who did it solely for financial gain.

Once you've figured out what your purpose is naturally you're going to become a busy man. Now you're doing something you're passionate about, it naturally becomes your primary focus in life. You have less time to chase tail since you're focused on your purpose. There's an upside to all this focus. Since you have a lot less available time for women you instantly become more attractive to women. An available man is an unattractive man because it signals a man who's chasing sex instead of chasing his dreams. An available man also is a turn off because it's a sign that other women aren't vying for your attention. Women want men that other women want. Point blank period! That's why every time you have a girlfriend or significant other it seems like every woman in the world wants you. Women are competitive that way. Women attract more women.

You don't have to fake being high-value if you are high-value but I always advocate fake it till you make it if you aren't exactly high-value yet. I advocate that because we men want sex now and waiting until we're high-value isn't practical. Becoming a high-value man can take months and in some cases years so act as if until then. Being a busy high-value man means it might take you a couple hours to return her phone call. Being a busy man means that you're not available the entire weekend so she either accepts your Saturday date or wait until you ask her out again. Yes, that means she might have to cancel plans to see you, that's the point! You want women to respect your time. The only way women will respect your time is if they know they can't have you anytime they get ready. You're not that available. This is why women will flake on a guy to see another guy. She has more respect for the second guy's time. She can either flake on you or flake for you, the choice is yours.

## EVERY MAN HAS ROOM FOR IMPROVEMENT

There's this perception floating around in the dating community that learning game and dating strategies is just for young men. That couldn't be the farthest thing from the truth. In matter of factly, I think it's an absolute necessity that every man keep his game Sharpe by always studying and learning game even if you've been in a long term relationship. Women are natural manipulators which means they naturally have a strategy to get what they want. Women learn at an early age that all they have to do to get what they want from men is show a little skin. This is done to get her the upper hand or power in the relationship. Men have to be up on game to counter a woman's strategy to get the upper hand in the relationship. The strategies I teach you in this book are to keep a woman chasing your validation. Another thing to consider is it takes game to keep a woman interest level high. Uncertainty is a woman's kryptonite. Uncertainty is the opposite of validation. Once you give a woman certainty the mystery and challenge are over and she starts to look for her next prey. As your feelings start to get deeper, if you're not up on game you tend to give women more certainty thinking that's what women want. Simple mistakes like this can be avoided if a man stays up on game. Unless a man can sleep with a hundred out of a hundred of the women he meets its imperative to stay improving his game.

## PERSONALITY

Charisma gets you laid more than anything else outside of status. Good looks and money get your foot in the door but rarely do they solely get you laid. Money can but only when it's a direct exchange. Don't get me wrong, getting laid is getting laid but money goes, looks fade, status fades but charisma is there to stay. Nothing turns women on more than a man with a smooth charming personality. Personality beats money and looks but nothing attracts women more than status. I think we can all agree rich celebrities attract more women than all the other attributes combined. The reason status is such an attractive quality is because it's the biggest form of social proof. Women want men that other women want and rich, powerful celebrities get their choice with women. When I was a teen, girls in high school would lust over me but once they got a glimpse of my personality they would get turned off. I would get overly excited at that sight of seeing women physically attracted to me. I would act childish and turn the women off. I learned the hard way a quiet more mysterious approach was best. Being mysterious gives women something to think about since you're not blabbing your mouth telling her your life story. Women like discovering you slowly over time. So you should let a woman do most of the talking by asking HER questions.

One of the biggest components to personality is seductive charm. Seductive charm is that cool laid-back demeanor that gets a woman in the mood. Being goofy and corny are the opposite to seductive charm. You're more inclined to turn a woman off opposed to turning her on acting goofy. You can be funny but not goofy. Women love a man with a sense but hate a goofy corny man. Keep it sexy and charming.

You can't change your personality, that's a fact, but you can modify it a bit until you get what you want. A lot of people would say this is being fake and maybe they're right, but men need to take a female's perspective to dating sometimes. Women wear pounds of makeup, push-up bras, girdles, eyelashes, weaves, etc. to enhance their beauty. They do all this to attract the highest quality mate they can attract. Men need to do the same. I'm tired of men taking the high moral ground. I don't condone lying about finances, career or having kids but if you're naturally a corny guy maybe modifying your personality for a month until you get what you want is ok in my book. Now this approach won't get you a wife but it'll get you plenty of sex.

## STATUS

When it comes to attracting women there is nothing more attractive than a high value male with status. The primary reason is because women are constantly trying to expand their social circle. Women are very sociable creatures and a man with a large social circle offers her the opportunity to increase her social circle. Also women are very competitive and love to show their girlfriends their high-value man. Women love to rub in their girlfriends' face how much money their man makes, how many friends he has, how connected her man is or how many employees he has. That's why I emphasize getting on your purpose so much. If you're on your purpose eventually you'll have more status and become more attractive without even trying. You should be constantly trying to expand your social circle not to get women but in life it's not always what you know but who you know.

## RESOURCES

We all know that women love a man that can provide. Resources are very important to a woman because it lets her know that if she chooses to have an offspring with a man he'll be able to provide. While that is all good and dandy for the female it sets you up to get used by a woman if you're not careful. Most men don't care how they get sex as long as they're getting sex. Sex is good but it's much better when you're having sex with a woman who genuinely likes you. She's not going to just lay there like a dead dog, she'll actually participate. I think it's fair to mention that there's nothing wrong with a woman wanting a man with resources. Society has put a high price on vagina and women know it. Feminism has taught women to place a high price on their vagina so it's in a man's best interest to increase his resources if he's truly interested in attracting a high-quality mate. Just like it's in a woman's best interest to stay fit and sexy if she wants to attract a high quality mate.

## PURPOSE

We all love money. Money offers freedom and opportunities. I'm all for making more money but what I really encourage is to find something you love to do and monetize it. They kind of go hand and hand. You can make money doing something you can barely tolerate or you can do something you love to do. The choice is yours but I'll say this, it's a lot easier to make money doing something you love to do opposed to something you can barely tolerate because you'll work longer and harder if it's something you love to do. Nobody has to put a gun to your head to go to work if you're doing something you genuinely enjoy doing. Thanks to social media its easier than ever to promote your business. When I was younger it was nearly impossible to start your own business because marketing was very expensive. Thanks to the likes of Facebook, Instagram, twitter, YouTube, etc., anybody can start a business. Being on your purpose means sometimes your social life takes a hit, not just dating women but this also means spending time with friends, family, co-workers etc., also takes a hit. It means your sole purpose for getting up in the morning is to pursue your purpose. Now I get this is a dating book so I know you're wondering how this gets you laid. Being on your purpose leads to eventually making more money, more money gives you more confidence and options. This new-found confidence and swagger eventually leads to more women, simple as that. Also most people find a source of happiness when they're doing something they love opposed to something they're just tolerating. This happiness is what gives you the ability to be alone because no longer do you need women as your source of happiness you have your purpose for that. This new-found happiness gives you the ability to stand up to her shit test which causes her attraction for you to grow because you're carrying yourself as a high-value man. Focusing on your purpose also makes you unavailable. That unavailability makes you sexy to women because women instinctively know a focused man eventually will be a successful man. Now please don't misunderstand me by thinking you're going to create a successful billion-dollar business overnight. In most cases it takes years to develop a successful business. This is only more reason to find something you love to do because you're likely to give up if it's not something you have a genuine love for.

## HOW TO FIND YOUR PURPOSE

Finding your purpose is as simple as finding what you have a passion for. The problem comes when a man doesn't know what he has a passion for or hasn't figured out how he can make a living off of his purpose. The reason a man wouldn't know what he has a passion for is because he simply hasn't tried enough things in his life. You have to be willing to try new things to find what you have a passion for. How will you know if you haven't even tried? Try a variety of things. When it comes to monetizing your purpose you need to find someone who's already successful in doing what you're trying to do and copy their business model. I'm writing this book because every successful dating coach that I know has a book out. I simply copied their business model. Most men might find that they have two passions. How do you decide between two passions? What I suggest is to pick the passion that offers you the most financial freedom. Financial freedom has a different meaning to everyone but to me it means being able to make a living without having to be at a fixed location. Passive income is what every man should be striving for. Trading time for money is not the way to go. Working the hours of the day I choose to work during the day instead of when a supervisor wants me to work is financial freedom to me. Some men will have the problem of knowing what their purpose is but are unable to focus on it due to having to work long hours on the job. In a situation like that I suggest the man downgrades his lifestyle and take on more of a minimalist lifestyle temporarily to focus more on his purpose. That's a small price to pay in my book to do what you love to do for a living in my book. At the end of the day it's up to you to make your purpose the priority in your life not a priority in your life.

## THE DOWNSIDE TO BEING ON YOUR PURPOSE

I teach men to be on their purpose to find fulfillment in life outside of women to improve their living situation and happiness. Although in most cases this would almost certainly make you more attractive to the opposite sex, there is a downside. There are some women who punish men who have their stuff together. To a select few women they'll sleep with a handsome loser quickly and make the handsome successful guy wait for sex. These women will label you as a beta male provider. This simply means they're labeling you as a potential boyfriend or future husband. In this situation they want you to see them as respectable women and therefore they'll withhold sex from you. Women have two strategies they utilize to get a guy to make them their girlfriend. The first one is she'll withhold sex usually claiming to be celibate to get a relationship before engaging in a sexual relationship. The second strategy is she'll do the total opposite to get what she wants. This is when the woman will engage in sexual acts hoping to get the man sprung or attached to her sex. Once she has him sprung or attached she'll simply withdraw sex with an ultimatum to be monogamous or she'll walk. This is another form of a shit test. Most true high-value men are able to pass this shit test. This is when you see a woman engaging in non-committal sex with a man for many months and in some cases years without ever securing a commitment. Now if you're a man you obviously would prefer the latter. Which strategy a woman uses is totally dependent upon how a woman perceives you. If a woman perceives you as having many options, she'll try to get you attached or sprung but if she perceives you as having limited options she'll claim the celibacy route. Your social awareness indicates to a woman which strategy to use. If you're socially awkward than women will withhold sex if they want a relationship from you. If you're socially aware women will use the attachment route to get a relationship. You can fake high-value but you can't fake social skills. Having social skills is just what it says, a skill. As with any skill the more you use it the better you are. When a man is genuinely on his purpose his social skills can diminish. That's why I encourage guys to stay on their purpose Monday through Friday and to socialize on the weekend. Becoming a total recluse is not going to help you once you get back on the dating scene. So make sure you have a little balance in your life to keep your social skills somewhat Sharpe unless your purpose is just really keeping you occupied. If that's the case I wouldn't really worry about it because business comes first.

## BROS BEFORE HOES

I love sex just as much as the next man but as men there are rules we must follow. There's an unwritten code in dating that must be followed by all men. We don't sleep with our brothers' women past or present unless he ok's it. By brothers I mean men that are either family members or friends. Women will throw sex your way especially if they know you're friends with their ex. They might not even be attracted to you but it's not about attraction, it's about getting the narcissist validation of knowing she could get you to betray your friend for her sex. Sleeping with your friends' ex also displays a scarcity mindset. You're acting like there aren't four billion other women in the world. No need in losing a lifelong friendship over a piece of ass.

## LIFESTYLE OVER STRATEGIES

I want guys to look at this book as a lifestyle adjustment and not strategy adjustment. Guys will read this book and apply some of the strategies wondering why aren't they working? Well you get from the universe what you put in. If you're doing the "strategies" without truly being a high-value male you simply are putting fake energy into the universe. It's called the law of attraction. When I started using the "strategies" they weren't strategies at all. I was truly being a high-value male and genuinely couldn't respond right away to females' calls or texts. Logically you would think women would respond negatively to my slow responses but they didn't. Their interest would seem to go up. You apply the "strategies" and they don't always work for you the same way they work for me. That's because you're faking high value and not genuinely high value. The universe has a way of sorting these things out. To get positive reactions from the strategies I suggest you focus first on becoming a true high-value male and not some unambitious loser who's hoping to raise women's interest by faking high-value attributes. Women have hundreds of shit tests and eventually one will display if you're a true high-value male or a phony.

## THE FOUR MALE STRATEGIES

Every man has a strategy to attract and sleep with women. Maybe you don't necessarily look at it as a strategy so to speak but you definitely have a game plan you use to sleep with women. I've broken these strategies down into four categories. Here's the cons and pros to all four strategies.

## NICE GUY STRATEGY

This is the weakest strategy in my opinion. The nice guy wants to sleep with women just like the rest of us but he takes the best friend and plutonic friend route. The pro to this strategy is you spend no money. When you're a woman's friend she doesn't expect you to pay for her since you two are friends opposed to dating. The con is it could take you years to sleep with your female friends if you ever do, to be honest. In the past I've slept with my female friends but it took almost ten years. Even then it only happened after I raised my sexual market value by increasing my earning potential and even then it took them to be in a vulnerable state after a break up. Being a woman's friend kills your SMV in my opinion due to the fact you've relegated yourself to being a woman's friend to get laid and everyone knows it. All her friends and associates instantly lose any attraction if they had any to begin with since you're their friend's lap dog. Always let a woman you want to date her romantically and if she's not with that then take your rejection like a man, at least you'll have your self-respect and dignity.

## BETA MALE PROVIDER STRATEGY

This is the guy that wants to show a woman what kind of provider he could be. Don't get me wrong, I advocate using a woman's hypergamy nature against them but let them discover your success, don't lead with it. You'll only come off as a try hard. When I say lead with it I'm referring to picking a five-star restaurant for a first date. Trust me when I say the woman will appreciate the five-star treatment but her attraction and respect level drops because you're acting like a man who needs to put on a show to get a woman's approval. Nothing drops a woman's attraction faster than a man seeking a woman's approval. Never offer to pick a woman up or drop her off in the hopes of showing off your nice car. Women aren't dumb and she knows why you're being so generous. If she asks you to pick or drop her off then that's a different story. If you're a successful guy there's no need to lead with your success, women's hypergamous nature will lead them to try and find out your earning potential. In fact it might benefit you to downplay your success a little bit, this only makes her try harder to find out what you're hiding.

## HIGH VALUE MALE STRATEGY

This is the strategy I hope more men adopt only this isn't really a strategy, it's more of a lifestyle. When you live an alpha male lifestyle you live by your own set of rules and you have the ultimate abundance mindset. This means if a woman is not giving you one hundred percent cooperation you have the ability to walk away. This means you've mastered the ability to be alone. This means that if friends, family and the women in your life don't enhance or add to your life you have no issue cutting them out of your life. This means you don't have time to blow women's phones up or respond to text messages in thirty seconds. You're a busy man whose focused on his purpose in life and everything else comes in a distant second. The con to this strategy is that you will turn off women who want to be put on a pedestal. The fact that you aren't pursuing them day and night like the other beta males they will lose interest. High-value males could care less due to their abundance mindset. Women who are in their masculine energy will also more than likely lose interest simply of the fact they can't get the lead in the courtship or due to your high value mindset maybe you don't want to put up with their demanding attitudes. In any effect as a high-value man expect to turn some women off with your confident attitude. Most women today expect every man to grovel at their feet for sexual attention. The pro to this strategy is it raises more women's interest levels than not. When you encounter feminine women and you're on your purpose you'll raise their interest levels due to the fact you're a mystery. You're not readily available and since you're different you raise their interest level. You're acting like an equal and someone she can look up to. The funny thing is you're not employing a strategy. You're just a man with a purpose.

## DIRECT APPROACH

The direct approach is a controversial strategy. The main reason this is a controversial strategy to me is because we live in the #metoo era. My biggest issue with this approach is women are getting men locked up for all kinds of sexual harassment and walking up to a complete stranger insinuating sex could be considered harassment to some women. In life most people do things in extremes. Being a trainer at the gym I see clients who try to lose weight by cutting all their carbs out from the start. Needless to say they don't get the desired results. There's a balance with losing weight and there's a balance between letting your intentions known when dealing with women. I think men should definitely let women know they want something romantically with them to avoid women playing coy and using them for free dates but I think it's too extreme to be talking sex on the initial interaction. The pro to this strategy is you'll spend no money and give none of your non-sexual attention. When you're being direct from the get go means you're letting women know from the start, I just want a strictly sexual relationship. She can either agree or keep it moving nonetheless you haven't given her none of your non-sexual attention and spent no money on dates. The con to this strategy is that it'll only work on women who have a very high initial interest in you. In other words if a woman only sees you as a seven on a scale of one to ten, you could blow any chance to raise the woman's interest level. The whole reason we even date women is to raise their interest and comfort level to engage in sexual intercourse with us. More times than not the average woman you meet is not going to have a crazy high interest level right from the start to sleep with you, so if you're applying more of a direct approach be prepared to lose a lot of women you could have easily slept with by raising their interest level on a couple dates. I like to call this leaving ass on the table. I'm totally against a direct approach except on vacation or something like that. In those rare situations I recommend using more of a direct approach because you're probably not going to have enough time to raise her interest level anyway with dates.

## WHY YOU SHOULDN'T BE WORRIED ABOUT WOMEN KNOWING MY STRATEGIES

One big question that keeps coming up is how good will the strategies be once more and more women find out about them? First off they're not really supposed to be strategies technically. In reality the strategies only work if they're your lifestyle, not strategies. It's vital for any man to genuinely be working on improving their life and SMV. Faking high value will only get you so far. For one when you're faking high value you'll be too attached to the outcome and too dependent on the outcome. Men who are on their purpose aren't concerned with a woman losing interest because he can't return her call in ten minutes. Men who are on their purpose aren't concerned with women who lose interest because he's not available for her whenever she wants him to. The only men who should worry about women knowing the strategies are men who are faking high value. If a woman knows you're not working on your purpose but for some reason you seem so busy, she'll more than likely think you're following some script pretending to have more value than you really have. On the other hand if you're genuinely on your purpose she'll know you're truly busy and not think you're following a dating handbook. Purpose fixes everything fellas.

## HOW TO ATTRACT ANY WOMAN

Some guys have this preconceived notion that there are different approaches or strategies to attract different ethnicities of women. The bottom line is this, it doesn't matter if a woman is Haitian, Portuguese, Italian, etc. It basically boils down to whether a woman finds you attractive and you make a confident approach. At the end of the day with any woman you meet the progression to sex goes as follows. Man meets woman, woman is attracted to man, man and woman exchange numbers, man sets date with woman, man passes all woman's shit test and raises woman's attraction, man asks woman out for second date, man passes second round of shit test, woman's interest rises even more, man invites woman back to home, woman accepts, man makes his move, woman rejects, man and woman go back and forth until the woman gives in and sex occurs. If the woman doesn't come back to your place on the second date then it happens on the third date. There are no special strategies to attract any type of woman you approach, period. Either there's attraction or not. Either you're confident or not. Either you have the game to raise her interest level over the course of a couple of dates or not. It's that simple. The same goes for bartenders, waitresses, airplane stewardesses, etc. It's all the same.

## THE DOWNSIDE TO SELF IMPROVEMENT

I think it's safe to say that pretty much any man who is walking the earth knows that improving yourself financially improves your possibilities with women. While that's nice and all, a lot of men tend to start to rely too much on their improved looks and finances. There's two steps to sleeping with women. That's getting your foot in the door with your looks and financial stability. Alpha males can get in with just looks while beta males need the financial stability element. Either way your foot is in the door. Unfortunately, this won't guarantee you sex with the lady. You'll still need to have the second element to sleep with women. It takes charisma and game to seal the deal. If the woman finds you very attractive but you lack the charisma you won't be able to sleep with her. If you have financial stability but lack game women would probably use you for financial support without sleeping with you. That's why

It's important to have game and a standard you live by. When you live by the three-date rule it prevents you from getting strung along by women. The three-date rule basically means that if you haven't slept with the woman by the third date you cut your losses and move on. At the very least cut out the dating part and just invite her over. Take the financial invest out of it. Men have to understand that self-improvement is an important point in building your rotation but it's not the end all be all when it comes to sleeping with women. Think of it like this, when a person goes blind their hearing improves. That's called compensation. When a man's finances improve most men start to rely solely on their financial success and start slacking on the charisma. While that may get you over with women who are primarily focused on a man's financial stability, that won't get you over with women who aren't solely focused on a man's resources. You're going to be leaving a lot of ass on the table so to speak. I'm about maximizing my whoring. I want to sleep with as many beautiful women as I possibly can.

## HOW TO GET LAID WHILE YOU'RE BUILDING YOUR EMPIRE

I advocate for men to focus on self-improvement to improve their SMV but let's be honest here, we still have needs. Losing weight and improving your financial situation can take a long time in some instances and telling men to wait until they've finished improving themselves to get laid is unrealistic. One thing you need to understand about some women is that they'll date you off potential but you have to be able to sell it. By sell it I mean you have to convince or show her that you have a plan and are focused to get there. Some women are willing to date off future potential earnings but not if she thinks its 20 years away. You have to convince her that it's not that far off and you're close to obtaining your goal. If you meet a woman and you tell her you just quit your job to start a startup it's a very good chance you never hear from her again. First off never quit your job until your purpose or passion has some kind of income coming in. You never know how long it'll be before you start generating income. Secondly, never let her know you're in the beginning stages. Tell her it's starting to move in the right direction. She can derive anything from that she wants but you're being vague for a reason. You're trying to string her along as long as possible so you can keep having sex with her as long as you can. Don't worry about feeling guilty either, it's her greed that's gotten her here. Women have been manipulating and using men for free meals and free attention for years.

Men complain about female hypergamy all the time but I don't advocate bitching about female nature I advocate using women's hypergamous ways against them. Sell her a dream and string them along as long as you can boys. Eventually after a few months or in some cases a few years she'll eventually catch on that her get-rich scheme is taking longer than she initially thought and walk. No worries, you've already gotten what you want. Time to manipulate the next GOAL digger. When I was a security guard in NYC I used to use this strategy a lot and it worked. I would tell women that I had my own security company and that I had a few contracts. They would then ask me why I was living in a basement in Brooklyn and I would say that I was saving to get more contracts. I told them I was hoping to get more insurance coverage to get bigger contracts. They always fell for it. Truth of the matter was it was hard to get contracts in the city and it took me like 3 years before I started making some money. I wasn't about to go 3 years without having sex and you shouldn't either.

## HIGH-VALUE MEN VS. FAKE HIGH-VALUE MEN

I advocate for men to get their stuff together. Getting your stuff together means getting your life in order. That means you have your own apt., car, job, savings account and good credit. This don't mean you have to have a 30-million-dollar mansion, a Bugatti or 2 million dollars in the bank. This simply means you have a comfortable living situation, reliable transportation and a few months' rent in the bank for emergencies. Saving for emergencies is essential because you don't want to be one paycheck away from losing everything. All those are essential for any man looking to have a very successful dating life but they are not what makes you high value. A high-value man is a man whose time is very limited. It don't matter why your time is limited, only thing that matters is that it is. I prefer for it to be because you're focused on your purpose, but it could be because you have a lot of friends or women etc. On the other hand, a fake high-value man is a man who acts busy but really has plenty of time on his hands. This is the type of man who returns a text message five hours later acting busy but in reality he's playing Madden football on PS4. I actually advocate acting high value until you get your purpose figured out but once you figure out what's your purpose you shouldn't need to fake being a high-value man anymore. You should be busy, extremely busy. Faking high value should be a short-term fix but not a lifestyle. Consider it a band aid. I want men focused on their purpose not faking like they're busy. Besides, men who are focused on their purpose and mission will have a confidence that can't be faked. You might can fake being busier than you are but you can't fake confidence. Confidence is something that can only come from genuine self-improvement. When you're out with these women and you're unsure of your future and where you're headed it's going to come out in the interaction with women. I say this because I know guys are going to read my book and think "hey, all I have to do is act busy, problem solved." Not so fast my friend. Being busy is only a small fraction to attracting women, you still have to pass their test and that only comes from genuine confidence. You can't fake confidence.

## TEN DATING COMMANDMENTS

Men should always have rules and boundaries they stand by. If you're a true high-value man you should have a standard you expect all women to follow. Throughout my dating life I've developed what I've called my 10 dating commandments. I don't bend or fold when it comes to my commandments. Every woman I date either obeys my commandments or I dismiss them.

### - NEVER LET WOMEN MOVE YOU OFF CENTER

Women can be some of the biggest trolls around. Women love to get under a man's skin especially when she knows you're easy to move off center. Typically, with most trolls if you don't react emotionally they stop trolling because what's fun about trolling if you can't get a reaction? Arguing with women also is feminine behavior. It leads to women moving into their masculine energy. This masculine energy in women comes out as bitching. Responding emotionally to women bitching only leads to eventually the woman losing interest. Always remain in a calm assertive tone when dealing with women.

## - NEVER RESPOND TOO FAST TO WOMEN's CALLS OR TEXTS

Responding too fast to women's calls or texts lowers interest because you're showing high interest. The best way to keep a woman's interest is to never let her know your interest level. When you're taking your time to respond to a text or call you're allowing your woman to wonder about you which only raises her interest. This shouldn't be too hard to accomplish considering you're supposed to be on your purpose not playing Madden faking high value.

## -ALWAYS CHECK YOUR WOMAN

Men must understand that the testing with women never ends. It's always ongoing even if the woman is head over heels in love with you. Women are backwards, the more you care the more they test. They have to make sure you're not getting booty whipped. She wants you to care but not to the point where she starts to run the relationship. When she tests you, you have to check her. If you don't this will lower her interest because you're starting to let her walk all over you. Even in this feminist society we live in today no woman wants to have a man who can't stand his ground. It makes her feel that if you can't stand up to her then how in the hell could you stand up for her if she was in some sort of danger? It shows a lack of confidence and a scarcity mindset. A lack of confidence is like kryptonite to a man. Nothing kills attraction worse than a man who loses confidence.

## - NO VALIDATION

Women love validation and hate it at the same time. What I mean by that is women love to hear how good they look but it causes them to lose interest because you've just killed the mystery of her wondering do you even like her. It's always better when the woman thinks she likes you more than you like her. You keep her submissive that way also. Complimenting women makes them look at you as more of a fan than a potential mate. Keep her chasing your validation and don't give it out so freely.

## - NO DATES AFTER THE SECOND DATE

We all know that women have no problem using men to pass time. It can be kind of difficult at times to tell what a woman's intentions truly are at times. Is she looking for free dates and attention or is she genuinely interested? Well one way you can find out is by not taking women out on dates past the second date If she still hasn't come back to your place by the end of the second date. If she has come back to your place by the end of the second date you can take her out one more time but if you haven't slept with her by the end of the third date stop taking her out. If you haven't slept with her by the end of the third date you simply invite her over so the both of you can cook dinner together. This will allow you to make your move. If you don't sleep with her by the end of this date cut your losses and move on. She's more than likely using you for free attention or her interest is extremely low. The only exception I would make to this rule is if she's offering to pay for a date. If that's the case she's probably just being careful but to be honest this is extremely rare.

## -KEEP YOUR NON-SEXUAL ATTENTION TO A MINIMUM

Women are notorious for using men for their non-sexual attention. Women need your attention for validation and to feel better about themselves. Keep your phone and text conversations to a minimum. Don't let women use you while they sleep around with other guys. If she's not sleeping with you best believe she's sleeping with someone. Men have to learn that our attention is worth something. Women have the mindset that their sexual attention is worth something. Men have to have the same mindset when it comes to our non-sexual attention.

## -NOTHING COMES BEFORE YOUR PURPOSE

As a man nothing should come before your passion and purpose. At the end of the day women come and go out of your life but your purpose is there forever. Women have the edge on men due to Mother Nature giving them a vagina. Your purpose is what evens the playing field. A man without a purpose or a man who's not focused on his purpose is a man with a void that needs filling usually by a woman. Most men without a purpose repulse women because they're way too needy. In reality a man could have many more options if he'd focus more on his purpose and less on women.

## -NEVER BE A WOMAN'S FRIEND

When you agree to be a woman's friend you're essentially trying to backdoor your way into her pants. Women have no respect for a man who's willing to be her friend in hopes of one day getting a chance to get in her pants. Women know men who have options would never relegate themselves to being their gay male girlfriend. It's weak and show's no self-respect. If you want to sleep with a woman just be direct about your intentions. Let her know you only want something romantic with her. If she declines that's her choice but you have a choice also and your choice should be to keep it moving. Now don't get me wrong you can be friends with a woman but only if you don't have any romantic desires.

## -KEEP YOUR DATES CHEAP

Dating can be a costly thing if you're not careful about spending on dates. Spending tons of money on dates trying to impress women doesn't work. It only lowers their attraction because the mere fact that you feel like you need to impress her with a fancy date you're subconsciously letting her know that she's of higher value than you. You're basically being a try hard. I'm not saying expensive dates won't work but they'll only put you in the beta male provider category. You want to be in the alpha category, that's the guy she sleeps with who doesn't spend a dime or very little at least. Keeping dates cheap also makes it easy to pull out if you don't like the pace she's moving at or her attitude for that matter.

## -NEVER ASK A WOMAN FOR A RELATIONSHIP

Men with options have a natural tendency to play the field as long as possible, women know this. A man asking a woman for a relationship causes two problems. It's asking a woman for something she's not ready for yet. Women generally take longer to develop those feelings of wanting a serious relationship. Most men are ready to get married if the woman is a ten on a scale of one to ten. Women typically need more before they're ready to settle down. It also shows a scarcity mindset which is always a big turn off for most women. Women are the gate keepers to sex and a relationship. Neither happens unless the woman says so. Men just have to carry themselves as high quality men and let the woman do the choosing.

## LOW TOLERANCE

The first step to becoming a high-value man is to develop low tolerance for women's crap. Thanks to feminism women try to take the lead from the start these days. To gain respect from women they need to know from the start you will not be tolerating any BS. Women need to know that you'll walk in a moment's notice if they misbehave. As with most things in life women respond to action not threats. It's been times in my life where I would break up with women only to have them beg me back. It's easy to make a woman submit once she's begged you back because now she sees you don't do idle threats. Low tolerance means I run the ship. The woman follows your lead. The funny thing is feminine women want to be led by a masculine man. Only women in their masculine energy try to lead men. Only men in their feminine energy with a scarcity mindset would allow a woman to lead them. Due to feminism there are a lot of men in their feminine energy, unfortunately. The main reason I'm writing this book is to help men be men again. Too many men are in their feminine energy. Hopefully this book starts to change this. Let's talk about some of the things you should have low tolerance for. The number one thing you got to make women respect is your time. Showing up late for dates, flaking on dates last minute are both examples of a woman not respecting your time. If a woman flakes on a date with you make sure the next couple of dates are at your house. If she shows up late for a date, make sure you check her and she buys the first round. You have to let women know you're a busy man and you don't wait on people. Now this is where being on your purpose comes in handy. If you're focused on your purpose and not at a woman's beck and call she'll already know this. She'll be on time and excited to see you because she doesn't know when or if she'll see you again. When you're readily available women tend to think your time is easy and abundant. Always present yourself as a high-value man, that way women always respect your time. Women can tell how many other viable options a man has just by how much of her crap he tolerates. These test women give men are commonly known in the dating world as shit tests. Basically, the more shit you take from a woman the less value she gives you because a man who takes crap off women obviously doesn't have many other viable options because if he did he would stand up for himself. A woman can never love you if she doesn't respect you. If it's love you're looking to get from women then you have to earn her respect first. Always stand your ground with women.

## INVESTMENT

Dating can be very time consuming and expensive. I advocate keeping your time and financial investment very low. Women can be very fickle. One minute they're all over you, the next moment they're not returning your calls. Now to be fair this is mainly due to men losing their way by focusing on the woman more than their purpose but none the less it's still frustrating. Unless you're a seasoned dating expert you're going to waste a lot of time and money with women who never really had high interest in you to begin with. You're going to run into women who only use men for free dates and attention, but you can minimize the damage by following my three-date rule. Women need men's attention. Attention gives women the validation they need to feel beautiful and wanted. Most women on the outside carry themselves like they're very confident but on the inside they have very low self-esteem. Women develop this low self-esteem from comparing themselves to the supermodels on magazine covers and other beautiful women. Also women know what they look like first thing in the morning before they put on their "mask." A female's mask is makeup, eyeliner, weave, girdle, etc. Women use these things to hide their flaws and raise their sexual market value. Women instinctively know that most men are only concerned with looks, so women know in order to attract the highest quality man they can is to look their absolute best. Men should do nothing to alleviate women's fear of not looking good enough. Never give a woman your validation. Giving women validation only makes them take you for granted. You always want a woman to wonder how you feel about her. This anxiety is what causes a woman to develop feelings of attraction for you. Always keep the initial dates as cheap as possible. Giving women fancy dates right from the start also makes women think you're trying to impress them. Essentially what you're doing without knowing it is telling the woman she's of higher status than you. You need to send the signal to the woman that you're good enough as is. She needs to know that you're a high-value man with options and you don't need to impress women with fancy dates. Women don't date guys who they perceive as having lower value than them. If you don't remember nothing else I teach you in this book, always remember this. WOMEN DATE UP. So always present yourself as a high-value male that has plenty of options. Keep your non-sexual attention to a minimum. Your non-sexual attention includes things like talking on the phone, friendly dates that lead nowhere are examples of your non-sexual attention. A man has to put value on his non-sexual attention. Women won't value your non-sexual if you don't. If you give it away freely women won't fight for it. Women need to know that when you call to set a date that they need to very damn well try and make it happen. If not, it might be a couple of weeks before your schedule clears up again, so they have a sense of urgency. Women do have plans sometimes, but you want to be the reason she flakes on the other guy. Don't be the guy she's flaking on because you're so predictable. Women get bored easily because they can get sex anytime they feel like it so a man who's not a challenge is boring to them. It's all a game to women so men need to stay focused on their purpose so women see them as the prize. Men who give women tons of their non-sexual attention usually end up in the friend zone. Women know men who have other female options would never give women the opportunity to use them for their non-sexual attention. Women think men who give their non-sexual attention away freely are not desired by other women. Men who value their non-sexual attention don't freely give it away.

## ALPHA MALES AND BETA MALES

The difference between an alpha male and beta male is simply mindset. To be more specific, an abundance mindset and the ability to enjoy being alone. Beta males typically need women's validation and hate being alone. That scarcity mindset and fear of being alone keeps a man from standing up to women. Contrary to what you see on TV, women like a man that's not afraid to check them. When a man fears being alone or doesn't have an abundance mindset he can't stand up to a woman due to fear of pissing her off and her leaving him. This weak behavior causes a woman to lose attraction. The only women who will stick it out with a man like this are women who are into their masculine energy with a feminist mindset. No woman in her feminine energy would tolerate such a weak man. Alpha males have an abundance mindset which comes off as confidence which is very attractive to women. It's not that the alpha is so confident, it's just that he really has no fear of loss due to his abundance mindset and the ability to be alone. This arrogance is what leads women to run to the alpha. If you want to become a true alpha male you need to adopt that kind of mindset. This mindset carries over into the real world. Alpha males typically work for themselves. The same abundance mindset that works on women is the same mindset that carries the alpha in the workforce. Beta males are burdened by the same scarcity mindset that hinders them with women.

As the old saying goes. Alpha fucks beta bucks. Women typically like dealing with the alpha males when they're at their hottest. That's usually between the ages of 18-28. Once they reach their late 20's and early 30's they start looking for the beta male providers. They now realize that the alpha is only interesting in sleeping with as many as he possibly can. The unattractive or no charisma beta male now looks like a winner. The out of prime female biological clock is ticking and she wants kids and marriage but here's the thing, they'll still cheat with the alpha on the side from time to time. Beta males need to understand something about women. They still need a man they can look up to from time to time. Beta males let their woman lead the relationship because they've let the woman get the upper hand in the relationship through female manipulation. Women like a strong masculine man that takes charge, unfortunately that's usually an alpha male. So the woman has the choice to be with an irresponsible or non-committal alpha male who lights her fire or a weak beta male who lets her run the relationship. Who does she choose? The answer is usually both. There's a reason most beta males feel so insecure all the time. Deep down they know their woman desires a more masculine man. These insecurities usually lead the beta male to ruining their relationship. The beta can tell somethings up but just can't catch it. That doesn't stop him from constantly showing the insecurities that eventually push her away.

Few men are born alpha. Me myself I was a certified beta male up until I was 27 years old. At the tender age of 27 I had an epiphany. I simply realized I didn't need to constantly have a girlfriend in my life anymore. I got comfortable being alone. Even before finding my purpose I was comfortable being alone. Finding my purpose has really helped me feel more comfortable being alone. Being on your purpose occupies a lot of time. It can keep you from spending money frivolously on stupid things like going out to clubs and online dates with less than attractive women. I've mentioned being on your purpose quite a few times in this book and That's for a reason. Being on your purpose and mission in life sets everything in order. As the old saying goes: PURPOSE FIXES EVERYTHING. You can't start to be an alpha male until you've learned to be alone. That means that unless a woman is 100% of what you want you have the strength to keep it moving. That's why I'm single, I haven't met the perfect woman for me. Does she exist? Maybe, maybe not, so until that time I'm perfectly fine staying single and mingling.

## MASCULINE AND FEMININE ENERGY

Perhaps the biggest turn off to a woman is a man in his feminine energy. A man is supposed to stay in a strong masculine state. That means never letting a woman or anything for that matter get you rattled. A masculine man always remains calm. Getting emotional or moving off center means you're moving into your feminine energy. I think it's safe to say that every man gets emotional from time to time. That's because men and women both have masculine and feminine energy. The problem comes when a man moves too far into his feminine energy and the woman moves too far into her masculine energy. Some women naturally carry more masculine energy but more times than not it's due to feminine men. A man in his feminine energy moves a woman into her masculine energy. If you have a girlfriend or wife right now and she's acting bitchy and you're looking for someone to blame, go take a look in the mirror. It's all your feminine behavior that has her acting bitchy. Being bitchy is a female's version of masculinity. Never let a woman lead the relationship. That's a sure-fire way to move your woman into her masculine energy. A man should always lead the relationship. That means you make the plans for outings, etc. You lead, she follows. Never yell or argue with women, that's feminine energy. Being too far into your masculine energy also could lead to your woman losing sexual desires for you. When a woman is having sex with you she's in a submissive position. It's practically impossible for a woman who's not submissive to her man to submit to him in the bedroom. If you want your woman to submit to you in the bedroom then you better damn well make sure she's submitting to you outside of the bedroom, it's that simple.

## DEVELOPING A MASCULINE FRAME

One of the biggest components to being successful with women is developing and maintaining a masculine frame. You can't just wake up one day and become more masculine. This is years of learned behavior. The best way to become more masculine is to hang around more masculine men. We tend to mimic the behavior of those around us. This is how we develop an accent. Once you start to live around a group of people long enough you start to adopt their voice pitch. That's how much we adapt to what's around us, our voices change to match our surroundings. We live in a society where a lot of men, especially black men, are raised by women and thanks to feminism even the men who were raised with the father in the household the mother generally runs the household. We are what we hang around guys. If you want to be more successful, hang around more successful people. If you want to reach your fitness goals, you need to hang around people who are living a healthy lifestyle. If you want to develop a masculine frame, you need to hang around masculine males. Developing a masculine frame is one thing but it's a whole other ball game to maintain it when you're out with the woman of your dreams. In a situation like this the only way you're going to be able to maintain this masculine frame is to genuinely believe you're entitled to this woman. It's natural for a man to turn into an entertainer or as I like to call them "a dancing monkey" during the date. This comes from the deep-down belief that you alone is not good enough. You subconsciously try to compensate for this lack of SMV by becoming her entertainer for the night. This is where the self-improvement comes into play to increase your confidence and you get a sense of entitlement. That sense of entitlement is going to turn the woman on. Women date up not down and becoming her entertainment for the night is a one-way ticket to the friend zone. Women can always tell when a man is compensating. Being a try hard is definitely not the way to go.

## VALIDATION

It was once upon a time that a man could give a woman a compliment. That day is long gone. Today, that's considered weak behavior.

Don't get me wrong, women like compliments just like they always have but the difference is thanks to social media women don't appreciate it. Social media has devalued a man's compliment and validation. Here's the thing, women tend to date up. Complimenting women is a sign of lower status. You're subconsciously communicating to the woman that you usually don't date women of her caliber. Essentially, you're saying I'll do anything to get a date with you your majesty. I'll do anything to make you happy your highness. If you don't remember nothing else said in this book always remember this: If you treat her like a celebrity she's going to treat you like a fan. Most women biologically can't be attracted to a man she perceives as lower class unless she thinks of him as a provider. That's a beta male provider to be exact. That's the old beta bucks, alpha fucks coming back into play. Never give a woman your validation. You want her to chase your validation, you don't just give it to her. Women have very low self-esteem for the most part. They get their self-esteem from men's attention and validation. Men's attention is validation to a degree. That's why you don't want to give women a lot of your non-sexual attention. When you give women a lot of your non-sexual attention you're basically saying you're more important than my purpose, friends and family. A woman should rank about 4th or 5th in your life priorities. You want a woman to look up to you, not the other way around. Always let a woman wonder where you stand as far as your feelings go and stay unpredictable. A predictable man is a boring man. When you're boring this will cause the woman to purposely cause drama or pullback to stir things up a bit. A predictable man never gives a woman a reason to engage her feelings. Women love a mystery. A man that doesn't give a woman his validation is very unpredictable. That's why it's easier to keep the women you have low attraction for instead of the women you have high attraction for. You're constantly validating the ones you have high attraction for without you even knowing it. From the way you look at her to the way you constantly want to touch her. When on a date keep your hands to yourself. If she's not wondering whether you like her or not, you're losing. On dates keep your hands to yourself. Don't gaze into her eyes all night displaying your high interest. Returning her phone calls in 2 minutes. These are examples of high interest. Displaying high interest is validation to women. Never do anything that displays your interest level. To be on the safe side it's always best if a woman thinks she likes you more than you like her.

## WHERE TO MEET WOMEN

The biggest mistake I've seen men make on the dating scene is leaving the house looking for women. I think it's safe to say that everybody knows you never find anything when you're looking for it. The best mindset is to just be out enjoying your life and not looking for women. Myself, I just let women do the choosing. Now when I say choosing I don't mean I expect women to come up and approach me. I simply mean I wait for IOI, or indicators of interest. These IOI's can be subtle so you must be observant. some of these IOI's include a woman staring at you, coming and standing near you and making conversation about nothing. The reason I prefer to wait for choosing signals is women will use you for free dates and attention. In my experience women who are sending off IOI's are genuinely interested, not trying to use you. Now you do have your share of attention whores, but they usually reject you once you make an approach. They only wanted your validation. At the end of the day women do the choosing. By that I mean us men would pretty much sleep with anything moving. It's women who are quote unquote the gatekeepers to sex. That's why I said women do the choosing. Can you go up to a woman who hasn't displayed IOI's and get her? Of course, you can but I want men to just present themselves as the best candidate and let women do the choosing. Looking for women sends off this hungry scent that turns women off. You call it being aggressive, but women call it being thirsty. Appearing "thirsty" is a female repellant. Women prefer men who are already getting laid because it's an indication of pre-selection status. Women think "hey, if he's ok to other women he's ok for me." I didn't make women, if you don't like it talk to the man upstairs. A confident man who's out just enjoying time with his friends is attractive to women, not the guy who's going around in the club talking to everything with a skirt on. Trust me, women are watching. You might think nobody's watching, but women are intuitively that way. The worst places to put yourself in a position to meet women are places you naturally think are the best. Nightclubs, lounges etc., but in my experience, these are the worst due to the fact women typically visit these places to get their attention fix for the week or just have fun with their girls. The best places to put yourself in a position to meet women would be doing something you genuinely love doing. For example, if you enjoy car shows then go to car shows. You're not going to the car show to meet women, you're going to the car show because you enjoy car shows. Now if by chance you just so happen to meet the woman of your dreams then that's just a good byproduct. The bottom line is no woman is going to come by your house looking for you, so you have to be out the house. Doing activities you love to do puts you in a position to meet women without looking for them. Notice those other places are locations where women aren't getting jazzed up to get free attention from men. That's the point, you limit the chances of meeting an attention whore. Just remember no matter the location, never leave the house to look for women.

## IT TAKES WORK TO BUILD A ROTATION & HOW TO HANDLE REJECTION

For some odd reason some men think women are just going to fall from the sky. It takes hard work to build your rotation. It takes a lot of dates, a lot of going out to build your female roster. I can remember when I was a teenager going out trying to meet women. I would hit every shopping mall in town and walk around for hours approaching women. I never let rejections deter me from approaching more women. I would simply deflect the rejection, chop it up as an insecurity in the woman and keep approaching more women. I never took the rejections personal, I would simply say to myself something to the effect of "she's afraid of catching feelings for me" or something like that. Men have to understand you have to go through a lot of no's to get to the yes's. Building your empire and building your rotation are pretty much the same when it comes down to the amount of effort it takes to accomplish them. Neither is an easy task. If you're trying to build your rotation you should be out at least 5 days of the week. When I say out I mean just that, you're out living a social life of abundance. It's not that you're out to meet women, you're simply out enjoying your life putting yourself in position to meet women. You get what you put in. The more you get out, the more opportunities you have to meet women. This should be done after you've gotten your purpose off the ground of course. Maintaining a rotation is going to be just as much work if not more than it was to build your rotation. Sleeping with a lot of women sounds good to every man who hasn't done it but once you're sleeping with five, six or even seven women in a rotation it can be pretty exhausting. Make sure you're hitting the gym to maintain your stamina so you can maintain your rotation. Once you've gone through all the hard work of building your rotation you don't want to lose it because you're having a hard time pleasing so many women.

## DISSECTING THE FOUR FEMALE STRATEGIES

Men need to understand women have strategies just like us, meaning they have a game plan to get what they want also. I break these women down into four groups. Materialistic women, relationship women, attention whores and alpha seekers. The materialistic woman strategy may be the easiest to spot because usually their conversation is typically based around material goods, shopping, traveling and trying to gauge your earning potential. Common things you'll hear on a date with these women is where do you work, where are some of the places you have traveled to, which college did you attend, etc. They ask these types of questions because they're trying to determine your financial value. As an alpha male in training I suggest you play along and play naive. Remember your goal is to get laid, it don't matter how. In actuality these women are the easiest to sleep with in most cases if you know how to play it because they aren't really concerned with character, sense of humor, SMV etc.

Women seeking relationships tend to be the most difficult to sleep with. I break this group into two groups. Women looking for relationships before they have sex or right after sleeping with a man one time. My issue with this group is they tend to not be the most enjoyable group to be around hence why they're holding sex hostage to get what they want, which is a relationship. Truth be told if their personality was up to par they wouldn't have to hold sex hostage to get a relationship. The bottom line is these women have dated guy after guy only to still be single due to their personality. At the end of the day most men demand more than a fat booty to commit to a relationship. Unfortunately, there's always a beta male willing to play these women's waiting game, just make sure it's not you. The other group is the women who are looking for a relationship but they're willing to let things materialize. These women are more practical and tend to bring more to the table hence why they're not withholding sex. What you'll usually hear from these women is "are you open to being in a relationship?" They just want to know if you're even open to the idea of being in a relationship. They do this to keep from wasting weeks or months on a guy who isn't even open to a relationship.

The attention whore is in a class all by herself. This is the woman who loves to reach out and feed you hope but never makes dates. Her strategy is to give you just enough hope to keep you pursuing her. She just enjoys the free attention.

When encountering an attention whore employ my strategy of putting the ball into her hands. You simply ask her out and when she gives you her lame excuse you simply reply back with "hit me up when you have available time to hang out." Leave it at that, and when she hits you again, and she will, trust me, you simply talk for a couple of minutes before repeating the exact same thing again. She'll either make the date or leave you alone. Either way you win because you're not giving her your attention for free anymore.

If you're reading this book, then you're in luck. The alpha seeker is the female who is looking for true alpha male qualities. These women tend to shit test a lot to weed out the beta males. Beta males cannot stand up to their shit test. Only true alpha males can stand up to these levels of shit test. These are typically the hotter women also as they have the sexual market value to demand an alpha male. To be fair all women are alpha seekers but only a select few have the SMV to demand an alpha male just like only a select amount of men can demand a beautiful woman.

## COLD APPROACH

Cold approaching women in the streets without any choosing signals or IOI's can be one of the most intimidating things a man can do in the dating world. We all know women can be rude when a man approaches them in public. The biggest fear men have with cold approaches is not knowing how women will reject them if she's not interested. Will she get loud and cause a scene or even worse, just act like you're not even standing there? For those reasons mentioned a lot of men prefer not to cold approach women in the streets anymore. Most men these days prefer to do online dating instead of approaching women in the streets. As we all know online dating can be easier as far as initiating contact but keeping women online interested is damn near impossible due to the amount of choices women have online. That's why I prefer men to meet women in public and not online. Now for the record I prefer for a man to be focused on his purpose and to let life come to him. I just don't like the fact of chasing tail. I think I'm the king of my reality and to pursue women who haven't displayed interest is just not my style. With all that being said, there are times when you'll see an attractive woman at the mall, supermarket, etc. and there just isn't any time for her to send choosing signals. In those rare cases I'll make an exception and say it's ok to cold approach.

Now what men need to know about cold approaching is that attraction is not a choice. She's either attracted to you or she's not. There's not an approach in the world that's going to get a woman who sees you as a 2 on a scale of 1 to 10 to sleep with you. You need to be at least a 5 for your approach to mean anything. If you're a 5 on a scale of 1 to 10 your approach can be the reason you're getting laid in a couple of weeks or getting rudely rejected. The higher you are on that scale of 1 to 10 to her the more room for error you have in your approach. Now the approach I prefer is to go up to a woman and introduce myself. I then ask the woman her name and would she like to get a drink sometime. Remember now this is a cold approach for a woman who's in a hurry like the mall, supermarket etc. so I'm trying to get to the point quickly. This isn't a woman I'm cold approaching in the club because in a situation like that I'm not even cold approaching. In a club situation I would wait for choosing signals or IOI's. If you're cold approaching a woman in a social setting who hasn't sent you choosing signals, something I don't advocate, btw, you would obviously do a little more small talk than that. You could ask her "do you come here often?" or something to that effect. Now when you're cold approaching women you need to understand that they are observing your body language and voice pitch during your approach. Nervous body language is a definite turn-off. Nervous body language sends a signal to the woman that you're not on her level. Subconsciously when we approach a woman we feel like we're entitled to we're naturally calm and smooth but in that same situation when you're face to face with a woman you feel is out of your league or you feel you would be lucky to get you're going to be nervous because you're fearful of screwing it up. The biggest attraction for a woman is confidence. Confidence is a sign of your status with women. Women are attracted to men who they perceive other women want. Men who have options with women are naturally going to be confident due to the fact that other women find them desirable. These men naturally think, "hey, women find me irresistible." Men who don't have many options with women naturally think women don't find me that appealing. This doubt is what causes the lack of confidence or nervousness. The solution goes back to the self-improvement. The self-improvement is what gives you the confidence and swagger from the increased sexual market value or SMV. With the increase in SMV you'll now have the confidence and abundance mindset to approach women with the mindset of, I'm on your level, I deserve you, not I'll be lucky to get you.

## CHOOSING SIGNALS

High value men don't have time to pursue women with low interest. The problem with cold approaches are that they allow women with low interest to waste your time. When you cold approach a woman, you could know from the get go you don't stand a chance but since they have nothing better to do Saturday night they figure they're doing you a favor by allowing you to take them out Saturday night even though they have virtually no interest. This is the selfishness and narcissism of some women. There's a solution for women like this. It's called waiting for choosing signals. Women with low interest will not send out signals; unfortunately, attention whores will. The good news is attention whores typically want just your attention but at least attention is free. They simply want to get your attention long enough so you can give them validation. These women like to know that every man they encounter wants to have sex with them. Attention whores enjoy being desired. There are two types of attention whores. There's the kind that just wants your validation by flirting with you but will reject you when you make a formal approach and the other type is the one that will give you her number and try to use you for your non-sexual attention by talking on the phone. However, you'll notice you never seem to be able to make a date with them. They'll always ask to get back with you or can they check their schedule? The good news is attention whores typically will not waste your money taking them out. They will, however, waste your time entertaining them on the phone using you for your non-sexual attention. It's imperative for a man to be able to walk away once he sees these types of characteristics coming from a woman. She's simply not interested in you sexually. All these pitfalls can be negated if a man simply waits for choosing signals. Some of the choosing signals women send off are they'll stare at you, stare at you and smile, come stand right next to you to make your approach as easy as possible or come create some ridiculous conservation about nothing. These are grade A choosing signals. I don't believe in flirting because it gives women free attention. Flirting with women also shows a lack of confidence on your part to make a formal approach. That slight hesitation could and in most cases will lower the woman's attraction. My attention is not free. If a woman wants my attention it comes with a price and that price is sex in the future. So make a formal approach. Don't allow an attention whore to use you for your non-sexual attention. Women are the gatekeepers to sex, so it really doesn't matter if you're attracted to her because at the end of the day sex will only happen if she's attracted to you.

## ATTRACTING WOMEN WHO ARE OUT OF YOUR LEAGUE

It's impossible to attract women who are out of your league. The thought itself is a contradiction. The most attractive quality initially to women is confidence. How confident can you truly be if you believe a woman is out of your league? It simply can't be done. Approaching women who you feel are out of your league is a complete waste of time. Women have like a sixth sense detecting men who feel unconfident or not worthy. Women date up and a man who feels he has higher quality than the woman is most certainly not going to be nervous. He's going to have a calm smooth presence about himself because he genuinely believes that he deserves the woman. So what's the solution? The solution is to get working on yourself to where you feel entitled to that woman. This is where the self-improvement comes into play. I don't believe confidence and swagger just come from the thin air. You have to work on yourself to get the confidence and swagger to attract the quality of women you want. Now it's not the money or new wardrobe that attracts the women. It's the attitude adjustment that happens when a man feels good about the direction his life is headed. Most guys who read this book will say there's no woman out of their league. Well if that was the case why haven't you approached that hot waitress at the bar or that hot chick in your class? Deep down you haven't approached because you're worried about her attraction level towards you. When you feel entitled to a woman this thought never enters your mind. So we all meet or see women who we feel we might not measure up to. That hesitation is doubt, doubt is fear that she might feel she could do better. I advocate men to constantly work on their purpose, bodies and game until it is oozing out of their pores. This self-assurance is what it takes to attract the upper level women. Some men are born with this, unfortunately most men are not. In a perfect world every man would just naturally have this confidence and swagger about themselves but as we all know this is simply not the case. If it takes hitting the gym, improving your finances, improving your wardrobe etc., as long as you get that magical thing women love called confidence, it really don't matter how you get it as long as you get it.

## BEING DIRECT WITH WOMEN FROM THE START

There's this big debate going on in the dating and pick-up community on whether a man should be more direct from the initial pick-up. Here's my problem with this approach and strategy. If a woman has very high initial interest, then having a straightforward approach can work for you but if you're a five or six on a scale of one to ten to that woman, having a straightforward direct approach more than likely will turn her off. If all you want to sleep with is women with very high initial interest, I'm telling you now that you'll be leaving a lot of ass on the table, so to speak. We as men have a lot of things at our disposal to raise a woman's interest. We can use our charisma, humor, sex appeal etc. The whole point of going out on dates is to raise a woman's interest to the point where she wants to sleep with you. I've had a few one-night stands in my life. I've also had sex on the first date a few times also. All those women had very high initial interest. All I had to do was not talk myself out of the sex. You don't have to be a seasoned dating coach or have much skill to sleep with women who have very high initial interest. You wouldn't be reading this book if the only women you were interested in sleeping with were women with very high initial interest. The sole purpose of reading this book and applying the techniques and strategies in it is to learn how to raise the interest level of women with lukewarm initial interest and to be frank going up to a woman you don't know and using sexual innuendo is creepy and could be offensive to some women. Remember guys we're living in the #MeToo era. You don't need those kinds of problems in your life. Stick to a formal approach. Introduce yourself and ask her "what's her name?" Then ask her would she like to meet up for a drink sometime. If she says yes, simply exchange numbers. This kind of approach has worked for years, I don't see no reason to change it.

## WOMEN'S AGE GUIDE

There are different strategies for different age groups with women. Young women tend to be more visual and less substance than older women as far as the men they tend to like. When I say young I'm talking 18-28 years old. Younger women prefer alpha males over beta males. Younger women are not concerned at this point about finding a beta male provider as of yet because they're having too much fun sleeping around with alpha males. They prefer the alpha males because these guys are looking for the same thing most younger women are looking for, non-attached casual sex and excitement. Beta males can be boring and predictable. Alpha males give women the uncertainty that women need to engage their emotions. In a perfect world, women would be as logical as us but they're not. Women are emotional which means they have to engage their emotions from time to time. Without this engagement of emotions women simply can't build an attachment. Younger women aren't concerned with a credit score, stability, etc. They're more concerned with superficial Things. An expensive car, jewelry, clothes etc. are good enough for them at this point. In my opinion this makes them the easiest to sleep with. I don't advise men to bankrupt their bank account to impress some young hot 22-year-old but if your finances are in order then this is one of the perks to having your life together.

The next age group 28-38 years old is when a woman starts to seek out the beta male provider. Once a woman reaches this age the alpha male is no longer at the top of their priority list. Women know they're starting to lose their superpowers so to speak and now they're trying to land a beta male provider while they still have some beauty left. Women realize that the longer they wait the more of their standards they're going to have to lower to get a man since men are primarily physical. In other words, the longer she waits the lower quality of man she can attract, and by quality that usually means resources since she's now looking to start a family and settle down. In this age group a good credit score, home, stability in the form of a steady job. No startup companies will usually do at this point. Of course as with anything there's always exceptions, but typically this will be the case. You need to be steady in your career before these women will take you seriously. Don't get me wrong, they'll still step out with the alpha male from time to time but generally speaking they will not consider the alpha for anything serious outside of having sex unless he's an all-around alpha male. An all-around alpha male is an alpha male whose alpha with the ladies and an alpha male in the business world.

The last age group is 38 and over. To be quite honest most of these women are quite delusional. A lot of these women don't realize that they are past their prime. A lot of these women think they're entitled to a top notched man making six figures a year, six feet tall and a six pack. To be honest I don't understand why a man who was on his purpose and grind would take an older woman seriously. Let's think about this for a second. This is probably the same woman who didn't even notice you when she was young and hotter. She was too busy screwing the alpha. Now that she's past her prime she wants you to come in and save her. Now the tables have turned so to speak and now you have the higher sexual market value. You should be pursuing hotter younger women. Let her go find a grandaddy to be her beta male provider. Don't let women who didn't even notice you when you were younger use you for your resources and stability now that they're past their prime years. The only caveat I would make in this situation is if it's a pure sexual relationship.

## WHEN TO CALL

Getting a woman's number is only the beginning of the challenge to having sex with a woman. It takes confidence to get a woman's number but unfortunately a woman wants to test your confidence even more. She needs to find out how many other female options you have. I know you're wondering how she's going to go about doing this. Only thing a woman has to do is just be a little difficult. Men who have options don't tolerate women's crap. Men with options don't call the next day, they're too busy conquering the world. Men with options have other women they're already dating. Men with options can't just fit a woman on their schedule on a whim. It could take a man with options anywhere from a week to a month to make the initial call or text. I know what you are thinking, "Isn't the woman going to be upset?" That's just the point, men with options don't care. Men with options could care less that some woman they haven't even been on a date with yet is butt hurt they didn't call or text right away. Men with options could care less. Another point to make is women who are secure about themselves aren't going to care you took so long to respond back. Women with a healthy self-esteem and social life could care less how long it took a man to make the initial call. If a woman don't want to go out because you took a little too long to call her just know that woman did you a favor because it's a good chance she'll be insecure and needy throughout whatever kind of relationship the two of you would have. Let's hypothetically say you don't have a busy business or social life, you know my motto: FAKE IT UNTIL YOU MAKE IT. Remember guys, availability is an attraction killer to women.

## SETTING THE DATE

After you've made the call you still have to do one more little thing: SET THE DATE! Women love trying to get to know a man over the phone, don't let them, though. It kills the mystery and attraction. If you talk to her too much over the phone what's the point of going on the date? You need to know how to set the date and get off the phone quickly, otherwise a woman could become bored with you or even worse, use you for your non-sexual attention by just wanting to talk on the phone. The initial phone call should be no longer than 10-15 mins just to get somewhat familiar with each other, any longer could kill the mystery. Besides you're a man on his mission in life, you don't have loads of free time for small talk. Ask her what's her availability this week? Don't ask her if she's available Saturday or anything like that because if she's busy Saturday you run the risk of looking too available when she counters with another day. You want women respecting your time and this respect is earned by not looking like your time is easy and abundant. That's how flakes happen. If she's unsure of her schedule, let her check her schedule and get back to you. Do not, I repeat, do not call or text her back to check to see if she's checked her schedule. If she hasn't gotten back to you accept it as her having low interest and just move on. She did you a favor. She could've used you for free drinks but instead she just didn't respond back. Better to never sleep with her than to never sleep with her and lose 40 bucks. After you've set the date tell her you'll think of someplace nice, but you won't tell her where. Tell her it's a surprise.

## CONFIRMING DATES

There's a reason you didn't tell her where. You're saving that to confirm on the day of the date. We all know how inconsiderate a woman can be when it comes down to a man's time. Women will flake on a man at the last moment with no hesitation or warning but confirming dates on the day of seems so unconfident. It looks like you're used to getting flaked on. That's an attraction killer because women could interpret this as you're a non-select man. A man who women flake on at the last minute. Does that sound high value to you? If you were an attractive woman with options would you want to date someone like that? So withhold that bit of information until the day of the date. So the proper way to confirm a date is on the day of the date send the woman the location, time and ask her does that work for her? The reason you ask her if that works for her is because you want her to give you a response. If you don't ask the question "does that work for her?" she could just be blowing you off and you'll never know it until she doesn't show up for the date. So be sure to include that question to illicit a response. Another reason you don't want to include the location during the initial phone call is because some other guy could come along and offer a better bigger date than you're offering. My objective is to keep my initial investment as low as possible as there's no guarantees you'll ever see this woman again after the initial date. Doing this not only keeps her wondering where you're taking her, which is exciting, but she could not want to go if it's not a fancy spot or if some other guy has a better offer to a better place.

## SHIT TEST

Women are like sheep, they like what other women like. A woman could have low attraction for a man but if she notices other women find you attractive her attraction level goes up instantly. Understand this, women don't know your sexual market value. It doesn't matter if you're 300lbs, unemployed and living at home with your mom. If women see that other women find you attractive their attraction level will more than likely raise. If nothing else a man who's that desired will obviously display high confidence due to the number of women fighting for his attraction. Most women don't care if you have a six pack and a Bugatti if other women aren't vying for your attention her attraction will more than likely drop. She'll be able to spot this by how nervous you are and your inability to stand up to her due to your scarcity mindset which comes from other women not vying for your attention. So on the first date women are naturally inclined to put men through tests that are designed to test a man's value. High-value men can naturally pass these tests due to their abundance mindset.

Usually these tests start right away and when I mean right away I'm talking when you're trying to set the initial date. When you ask her, "what's her availability this week?" She might hit you with the old "we'll see" or "I'll let you know" crap women love to holler. You simply withdraw the offer and ask her to get back with you when her schedule clears. She'll more than likely show up late for the date. Back in the day I would always tell guys to check the woman for showing up late for the date by telling her first round of drinks are on you. I've recently modified my stance and I now tell guys to be the one who is late due to most women being late. Unfortunately, some women will still be late due to their arrogance so if that's the case you simply tell her "first rounds on you." Understand guys these tests are subconscious which means she's not even aware she's doing them. Women don't sit at home and come up with these tests. Somewhere along in the night she'll probably test again. She'll probably try to get you to do something you don't want to do. I once had a woman on a date ask me to open her car door for her. Don't get me wrong, if you open car doors then by all means open women's car doors but if that's not something you do and you're only doing it because she suggested it then you're not being true to yourself and you're going to lower her attraction level. High-value men don't have a fear of loss and therefore are not concerned with upsetting women. I had sex with that woman the same night and that was a first date. My arrogant attitude probably turned her on. These tests are easier to pass when you have lower attraction. The true test comes in when you're on a date with a woman with whom you have a higher attraction. Somewhere along the date she might test you by trying to move you off center. Basically trying to piss you off by being negative towards you. She'll probably say something to the effect of "where did you get that shirt?" She asked you that to get under your skin or to see if you start doubting yourself. When a woman trolls you, you troll her back. You could say something to the effect of "this is my favorite shirt, I wore especially for you." Point being, don't let them see you sweat.

## SHIT TESTING WOMEN

Here's the kicker guys, you can test women also. Same rules apply, you're on the lookout for insecurities. Our strategy is similar to women's. When you're on a date just simply withhold your interest level. Insecure women when they can't tell what your interest level is you'll more than likely never hear from them again. The fact of the matter is since you're not displaying high interest level the uncertainty of your interest is too much to handle for them, you'll simply never hear from them again. I say good riddance. Insecure women need constant reassurance that you're truly into them. You can never compliment them enough, call or text to much, etc.

No matter what you do they're never satisfied, so unless you're looking for a woman you got to text all day you would want to weed this woman out anyway. Another great way to weed out insecure women is by waiting a week to call after the first date. Insecure women will immediately interpret this as low interest and not respond. Confident women will think "hey, maybe he's busy, he'll contact me when he get a chance." Confident women respect your time and let you focus on your purpose. Insecure women need to get a text or call from you every hour on the hour. You'll never accomplish your goals trying to keep an insecure woman satisfied.

## MISCONCEPTIONS ABOUT SHIT TEST

There's a misconception percolating through the dating community. Men have this perception that women won't shit test men who are successful or on their purpose. This is totally untrue. In my life I've been shit tested more when I was successful than when I was struggling financially. The reason for this is women subconsciously know men try to hide insecurities behind their successes. There's an old saying women use when trying to describe men with nice cars. Women refer to those cars as an extension of your penis. They use this phrase because women know most men only get expensive cars to compensate for something. It could be lack of bedroom skills, charisma, game etc. I'm not telling guys to not get nice things out of fear of getting shit tested. What I am telling guys is that nice things don't make you immune to shit test. In fact, nothing makes you immune to shit test. Even if the woman has sky high attraction she'll still test your strength. The amount of shit test you get depends on if you're failing previous shit tests. If you fail one test you get another, fail that one and you get another one and so forth.

## FIRST DATE

The first date is the most important date you'll ever have with a woman. As the age old saying goes, you never can make a second first impression. This is the date where a woman typically puts you in a box. That box is the alpha male box or the beta male box. This is why I don't advocate a man taking a woman out for dinner dates. Dinner dates come off as if you're auditioning to be her beta male provider. I advocate asking a woman out for a drink. Asking a woman out for drinks screams fuckboy aka alpha Male. Unless you want a woman to lump you in with the rest of the losers in her beta male zone ask her out for drinks. At the end of the date always ask her back to your place. Nice guys don't invite women back to their place because they want to play it safe and not offend the woman. Alpha males don't care if the woman gets offended due to their abundance mindset. You can ask a woman out for drinks or invite her back to your place and it still won't make a difference if you don't pass her test on dates.

Being boring is a good way to never see a woman again. You want to talk but you don't want to become a dancing monkey. That don't mean you're sitting there like the terminator either. You want to maintain a masculine, calm and assertive frame. This is where being on your purpose and hitting the gym comes in handy. Doing the self-improvement gives you a sense of entitlement and confidence which is what you're going to need to maintain a masculine frame. When you're nervous, which comes from the mindset of feeling lucky and not deserving, it puts you in this corny dancing monkey mindset. You become her entertainment instead of her date and she can see it. Remember women date up not down. Being nervous is an indicator to her that you're of lower status and not accustomed to women of her level. Stick to light hearted topics like her hobbies, favorite restaurants, ounces etc. Stay away from politics, crime and things of that nature. Those things kill the vibe and mood. Don't go for the kiss on the first date. I believe that reveals your hand too much and by hand I mean interest level. You want a woman wondering whether you even like her over the next few days. That anxiety and uncertainty is what causes her attraction to raise. Women like a man who's a challenge and a mystery. The only time you should go for a kiss on the first date is if when you invite her to your place and she accepts. Then I advocate not only going for the kiss but to also try and seal the deal.

## CONVERSING WITH WOMEN

So you've met the woman of your dreams and played your cards right setting up the date. She tried the old "we'll see" when you tried to set the date, you passed that test. She tried changing the day, you passed that test. She tried changing the time, you passed that test. You're prepared for all the tests she's ready to throw your way on the date. You're ready to show her you are no pushover. While that's all good and dandy it takes more than passing shit tests to keep a woman's attention. Being able to hold an interesting conversation is a key component to sleeping with women. If you can't maintain an interesting conversation but also keep the sexual energy by maintaining your masculine frame her attraction level will drop fast. You don't want the conversation to take on a friendly vibe; voice pitch or tonality is key here. Body language is also an important component; are your body movements friendly or of a sexual nature? This is also where the self-improvement comes into play. If you feel entitled to the woman, it's easier to maintain your frame but if you feel lucky to be on a date with her you're going to be nervous. This nervousness is going to cause you to lose your masculine frame and tonality, therefore the date loses its sexual energy. Being confident can be used to keep the sexual energy. Being arrogant causes the attraction to drop. The difference between a confident man and an arrogant man is that the arrogant man feels a need to brag about himself. This bragging or boasting comes off as being insecure. Boasting about yourself also makes you come off as a try hard who's not good enough as is therefore he needs to sell himself to the woman. Confidence is all you need. The reason for that is men who are confident remain smooth and relaxed. Being smooth and relaxed keeps the sexual energy. Being smooth and relaxed is what you need to maintain your masculine frame. Being corny or goofy is what happens when you're uncomfortable with a woman. She feels this and can sense she's out of your league or she'll be doing you a favor by sleeping with you. Like I've said before, women want men they can look up to. Passing shit tests is only one barometer women use to subconsciously judge men's SMV, they also look to judge a man's voice tone and body language to gauge your sexual market value. This is why the sexual energy is lost on dates. Losing your masculine frame is a sign of nervousness, nervousness is a sign of not being confident and we all know what being perceived as unconfident does to a woman's attraction level towards a man.

## HOW TO PURSUE A FEMININE AND HIGH INTEREST WOMEN

Let's be honest. Due to feminism most women are programmed to withhold their attraction level even if they have a high attraction level. Occasionally though you'll encounter a woman who hasn't succumbed to feminism or her attraction is so high she doesn't give a damn and will openly display her high attraction level. It's easy to spot also because they'll do silly things like actually showing up for the date on time or call you the next day following a date. I know right, go figure. A woman who actually shows up to the date on time. During the date you might notice her playing in her hair, she'll make physical contact throughout the night, ask you a ton of questions and shit test you very little if at all. At the end of the night she might make it so obvious she wants a kiss or even kiss you first. She might even tell you to call her when you get home or if you invite her back to your place and she comes that's an obvious sign of high interest. you want to make sure you recognize these signs because it's rare that you see them. It's rare to meet a woman with this kind of interest level. So you don't want to blow it because if you pursue these types of women the same way you pursue a woman who's following some rule book you'll turn her off. If she's displaying a high interest level, why would she want to date a guy who doesn't have the same interest level or at least close to her interest level? So if she's displaying high interest it's ok to pursue her a little more. The key word here is a little more. That don't mean you start blowing up her phone day and night because if you do that you'll lower her interest really quick. You simply want to reach out and make statements like "good morning, have a productive day." Notice I didn't ask her "how's her day going?" I simply made a statement. That statement might seem small, but it lets her know that I'm thinking of her at least. Make sure she is reciprocating. If she stops initiating contact, you simply pull back and by pull back, I mean you reach out once a week to make a date.

## WHO PAYS FOR THE DATE

Some men think its ok for women to pay for the first or second date. I totally disagree with this method. Whoever is paying is leading the interaction. Whoever is paying sets the time and location for the date. Asking a woman to lead can very easily put her into her masculine energy. It also could very easily turn her off because contrary to popular belief most women don't want to lead. If money is the issue I advise you to just keep it cheap. Men should always be in the leadership position. That keeps a woman in her feminine. When women are in their feminine energy they're much more fun to be around. Women can only have sex if they're in a feminine energy. When a woman is having sex with a man she is being submissive to him. Women can't submit to a man when she's not in her feminine energy. So it's very beneficial for men to keep women into their feminine energy if sex is their goal. Now there is a rare occasion that the woman will offer to pay. Usually this will come after you've paid for the first couple of dates and the woman has high interest. In a situation like this I would say its ok but other than this rare occasion I would say the man should pay. Not only does it put you in control but it's an unwritten rule that whoever asks who out should pay.

## HOW TO PURSUE FEMININE & HIGH INTEREST WOMEN

Screwing up with a feminine woman or a high interest woman with whom you have high interest can literally sting for years. The reason these sting so bad is because they don't come along that often. Maybe you meet women that have high interest in you but you may not share that same high interest or you meet women that you have high interest in but they don't share your high interest. So when you get both of these interest levels to be at a high level for both at the same time you know it's extremely rare so you don't want to blow these. The key is to pursue but to not make yourself too available. Women with high interest have a tendency to pursue you more than not so it's very easy to fall into the too available trap especially when you share the same high interest. Remember you can't make yourself too unavailable because that's a turn off to women with high interest because you're not displaying their same high interest. One of the biggest pitfalls with this is trying to see a woman twice in a weekend right from the very beginning. Only see women once a week in the beginning even if they're suggesting more of your time. Speaking for myself I never see a woman more than once a week. I want to keep a woman chasing my validation, but I do realize every guy reading this book might not want to stay single forever. If that's your situation I recommend at least waiting a couple months before seeing her twice a week. Since it usually takes women a couple of months to develop deep feelings this should be about the right time to allow her to see you twice a week. I said allow because only see her twice in a week if she's asking for it. You should never be the one asking for more of her time. Sometimes even when women want more time you still have to decline it. The age-old theory of women not knowing what they want kicks in here. On one hand she wants to see you more and on the other hand she is losing interest due to your availability. Another trap men fall into is the phone availability trap. It's ok to initiate contact a little more if she's displaying high interest but it's a fine line between showing interest to a woman and being too available. Rule of thumb to remember here is to never initiate contact twice before she has initiated contact and if she's texting you back and forth after the third text pull back a little and wait a few hours to prevent you from seeming too available. I made this mistake years ago and it taught me a very important lesson; never take women's high interest for granted and always keep my purpose first. I still have nightmares over one woman with a nice booty who had high interest for me and I blew it by being too available. Those type of mistakes last awhile sometimes.

## SUREFIRE WAYS TO NOT OVER PURSUE

In my dating life it's three situations where you can slip up and over pursue. The first one is double texting or double calling. This happens when a man reaches out to a woman either by text or call and can't get ahold of the woman. He then proceeds to reach out again before she can respond. This is classic over pursuing and uncharacteristic of a high value male. Guys need to understand that this is not always an indication of low interest. This could just be a test, or the woman could really be preoccupied. Men without confidence instantly think the woman isn't interested or losing interest. They let bad past experiences have a negative impact on their current situation. This is called having baggage. Another case of over-pursuing is when you reach out to set a date and the woman doesn't cooperate in setting a date. In a situation like this you simply tell the woman to reach out to you when her schedule clears up. After you've made that clear you simply walk away. You aren't going to call in a day or two asking her "has she figured out her schedule yet?" and you aren't going to wait a couple weeks to try again. If she never contacts you again, you simply move on. Now you know for sure she had extremely low interest. Now beware, sometimes these women will reach out again and try to get your attention but still won't make a date. She could be an attention whore or keeping lined up as a backup plan in case whatever she has going on fizzles out. Women generally test the water so to speak when their current lover or boyfriend is starting to lower their attraction one way or another. When a woman disappears on you then reappears you're never going to treat her like Cinderella. Always just invite her over to your place. Tell her to bring something like wine or some alcohol so she's invested. If she declines your invite end the call abruptly and tell her to keep in touch. Even if she calls you again you don't ask her out. You've done all the pursuing you're going to do. You're not going to chit chat with her all night either. Exchange a couple of texts or words if she called and get off the phone. Do that every time until she either makes a date or leaves you alone. The last situation of over pursuing is when a woman flakes on a date with you and doesn't try to reschedule. In this situation you tell the woman that you understand and to reach back out to you when her schedule has some free time. It's likely you never hear from her again. That's fine, at least you have your self-respect by not over pursuing. Women are fickle creatures and can lose interest easily. Over pursuing is perhaps the biggest turn off there is. Men with options don't over pursue. They have too many options to chase behind women.

## THE SECOND DATE

Assuming the first date went well, it's time to think about the second date. Now timing here is critical. If you call too soon you look desperate but if you wait too long you could come off as uninterested. So when is the perfect time to call? Well I prefer to wait 7-10 days. Here's the thing, even just waiting 7-10 days will turn off some women. See, women have been told that they're some special angels that should be worshipped. Anything over three days won't be good enough for those princesses. The bottom line is most women want a man that is drooling out the mouth on a date. These women know these men will be easy to manipulate. I prefer women with their own lives. Guys must understand one thing, women can call you too!! See, despite what society says, its ok for a woman to call a man. This is where the abundance mindset kicks in. I'm a tell you straight forward right now a lot of women will be upset that you waited to call and probably not answer but my question to you is why should you care? Did she pick up the phone and call you? Aren't you valuable? Remember you're a high-value man that doesn't live by anybody else's rules. Call when it fits your schedule to call. Once you've figured out when you're going to call it's time to set a date. When setting up the date always remember to ask the woman what's her availability. You don't want to make the mistake of asking her if she's available a particular day and she's not available. If she gives you a counter date you look too available if you accept. Secondly always be in control of the situation. Since you'll be the one more than likely paying you make sure you choose the location. If you let women choose not only do you look like you don't know how to take charge but you also run the risk of going over your budget. Remember you're trying to keep your investment as low as possible. Women are fickle; one minute they're all over you and the next they never want to see you again. If you haven't spent much money who cares; there's plenty of other women in the sea but if you spent a lot of money those things sting.

Once you're on the date the same rules apply. keep your interest level to yourself. If you did everything right on the first date to raise her interest level like passing her shit test and now that you're on the second date her interest level should be higher. Always remember, she's always going to test you. So you still have to pass her shit test on this date as well. by the end of the date you should know where you stand as far as her interest level goes by the way she's acting. She should be making body contact at this point, playing in her hair, etc. You might've saw this on the first date if her initial interest was high enough. Now that you've made it to the end of the date it's time to really check her interest level. Let's assume she didn't go back to your place on the first date as most women won't. What happens over the next few minutes will determine if you ask her out again or just move on. First, you're going to ask her back to your place and let's assume she declines. Well if that's the case you have to go in for the kiss. Listen carefully, if she declines it's time to walk away. Now understand this, some women just want sex and maybe she doesn't want a kiss. Well if that was the case then why isn't she going back to your place so you can make a move? So she clearly doesn't want just sex. She's obviously looking for something of more substance but how is she looking for more substance if she's not even willing to kiss? This is a woman just passing time until a guy she really wants comes along. This woman is more than likely using you for your non-sexual attention. I don't care how hot she is to you, you're obviously not that hot to her. It doesn't matter what's your attraction level if it's not mutual. You want a woman who gets wet at the mere sight of you, not a woman you got to beg to give you a kiss.

## CELIBATE WOMEN AND WOMEN WITHHOLDING SEX

Due to feminism women are more masculine than ever. This masculinity in women has caused more and more men to just look at women as just sex objects. This has caused many women to play the celibacy card. There are three reasons a woman would play the celibacy card. The first being that she's trying to rebrand her vagina like a brand new car. She's basically trying to roll back the odometer on her vagina. Unfortunately, women don't have a car fax but it's a known fact that the average woman has slept with more men than the average man at the same age so don't buy into the innocent crap. Another reason women claim celibacy is they've pegged you as a beta male. Due to social programming some women believe that any man who isn't breaking the law or is successful is a beta male. Anything short of a law breaker or loser is an honest beta male to them. Sometimes your actions could make her peg you as a beta male. Some examples of mistakes that could land you in the beta zone are calling a woman too soon after getting the number, responding to text too soon after she contacts you and trying to see a woman too much too soon. You should always try to carry yourself as an alpha male. Never act needy when dealing with women. Lastly, when a woman dates multiple men and is probably sleeping with at least one of them but due to her masculine non-submissive behavior none of them want to get in a relationship with her. In a situation like this a woman's only recourse is to retract her vagina from the market until she has a buyer. The fact that she had to resort to this tactic should tell you everything you need to know about her personality. When a woman has a laid-back submissive personality there's no need to resort to claiming celibacy to get a relationship. A woman's personality should be the reason you get in a relationship, not sex. She could never respect a man who agrees to that any way. How high could a man's SMV be if he agreed to something like that? Instantly a woman knows you have limited options and once she sees that it's over because when a woman doesn't respect you as a man with options she acts even worse. Odds are she is sleeping with someone but he probably only uses her as a sex option therefore she uses you for your non-sexual attention to fill that void she's not getting from the guy she's sleeping with. There are some women who do this as a form of shit test. These women think all men want is sex and they screen out men with this claim of celibacy. Me personally I don't waste my time on women like this. What if you shit tested her by telling her you were unemployed even though you weren't? Do you think she would stick around to find out if it was a lie? Exactly, so why should you stick around?

## ALPHA MALES DON'T KISS

Listen fellas, one of the biggest misconceptions in the dating community is that most women are looking for long-term relationships. This is perhaps the biggest falsehoods that lead beta males to failure when dating. This is something alpha males understand about women at an early age. If you don't take nothing else from this book you need to understand this one thing when dating women; most women you date aren't looking for a husband. Most are looking to just have a good time. Most are just looking for casual flings. When you're on these dates you need to have everything in place to seduce the woman back at your place. Beta males go for the kiss because they've been told that women are these innocent creatures that read the Bible all day. In reality a lot of women will lose interest if you're not progressing things to the bedroom. Some women are only looking for sex so if you try to kiss them they might reject you. Not because they're not interested but because they're not looking for anything intimate. I suggest always asking a woman back to your place and making a move there. You have two types of women you date. Women who are looking for something serious and women who are just having flings or casual sex. If you're out on a date with a woman who's looking for something special and you haven't lowered her attraction she'll kiss you. If you're out on a date with a woman who's just having casual flings and go for the kiss she's more prone to reject you, not because she's not interested but because she's not looking for intimacy. Always assume a woman is looking for casual flings, it benefits you either way. If it's a woman who is looking for a connection you're subconsciously letting her know that she doesn't have forever and a day to sleep with you. You're letting her know that the clock is ticking. The take home message here is to save the kissing for your girlfriend or wife.

## PREVENTING FLAKES

One of the biggest problems with dating in the social media dating age is flakiness. One reason women flake these days is the amount of attention women get online. Women get bombarded with messages on Facebook, Instagram, dating apps etc. You really have to have an abundance mindset these days. You could have a great date with a woman and never hear from her again which is why you should keep the dates cheap, by the way. You may have a great date with a woman and she'll flake on the next date. The best way to prevent a woman from flaking on you is to stay unpredictable.

When a woman feels she has the comfort of knowing she could have you anytime she gets ready she'll flake on you to do something else knowing you'll always be there waiting. You have to be a little bit more unpredictable than you have been if women are flaking on you. You want a woman excited to hear from you because you're so unpredictable. Your purpose should be your main focus in your life. A woman should be competing for your time not you just giving it to her freely. You giving a woman your time should be a reward not something she just gets freely. Another reason a woman flakes, and this is the one that stings the most, is she's losing or has lost interest. Unfortunately, one of the pitfalls to being too available is a woman slowly starts to lose attraction. You're starting to show weakness. You're starting to show signs of a man who can't resist her. You're starting to look like a man who's starting to make a woman his life. A woman doesn't want that pressure on her. What's the solution? Always keep your purpose and friends ahead of your woman in your list of priorities. Skip a week sometimes in between seeing your woman. Return her calls hours later. You're a busy man who's focused on his purpose, you don't have time to return calls in rapid speed. Keep a woman on her toes. A woman who doesn't know where you stand in relation to your feelings will never flake. In her mind she's thinking she barely has your attention as is, why would she want to do something as dumb as flake on a man who's not displaying super high interest to begin with? That's why it's best to keep your interest level to yourself, it keeps a woman on her toes. Never let a woman know where she stands and you'll never have to worry about a woman flaking.

## GETTING JERKED AROUND

One of the reasons I can write this book is because I've made tons of mistakes in my dating life. One of the mistakes I've made in my dating life is letting women jerk me around. Women will have you chasing your tail if you let them. I don't really blame women in this situation because men should have the strength to leave a woman alone if she's not cooperating. Women can only do what you let them do. Women enjoy jerking men around. They'll do something like tell you they're coming over after they leave work only to tell you they're going out with a friend after work now and that she'll come over after she leaves the happy hour spot. So here you are waiting for her at home checking your watch every five minutes staring at your cell phone only to tell you she's had a few too many drinks at happy hour and can she get a rain check? That's not low interest that's something far worse. It's called being jerked around. Getting jerked around is when a woman has lost all respect for you or maybe she never had it to begin with. A woman flaking on you is one thing, that could mean she's losing interest. Getting jerked around means she's lost interest or never had it. Never let a woman jerk you around. You'll only end up angry and frustrated. Getting jerked around is usually the result of not recognizing when a woman has low interest or losing interest. If your woman is flaking on you and you don't stand your ground, it'll only get worse. And by worse in the manner of you getting jerked around. If you let her flake once and just let it slide, she'll probably flake again and again and again. Getting multiple flakes is her way of toying with you. You probably recognize it but don't have the balls to walk away. Being a high-value man means recognizing your self-worth and value. If a woman starts playing games simply move on.

## TRYING TO IMPRESS WOMEN ON DATES

One of the biggest mistakes men make when going on dates is trying to impress women with their accomplishments and success. Yes, women prefer a successful man but it's null and void if you're bragging about it. You're pretty much saying "hey, I'm not good enough to attract you for the person I am so let me tell you all these wonderful things I've accomplished." That's a turn off because you're pretty much admitting that you're of lower value than the woman. Never forget women date up not down. Always carry yourself as a high-value man. Never discuss the other women you're dating trying to show that you're a pre-selected. It'll only lower her attraction. Women can tell if you're dating other women by how you carry yourself. Men who have options don't take women's crap, that's the whole point of shit tests. I remember being on a date with a woman and damn near begging her to let me take her home. The reason I wanted to take her home is because I wanted her to see my new Mercedes I was driving. Women are not dumb, they're actually pretty clever and manipulative. I'm quite sure that woman I took home figured out why I wanted to take her home so bad. I was trying to impress her with my car. This is one of the biggest mistakes I used to make back in the day. Let your accomplishments speak for themselves. Only talk about your accomplishments if the woman asks you a specific question related to your accomplishments. Never give a woman the "aren't you impressed" look afterwards either. Just look calm and keep the conversation flowing. If a woman whose obviously materialistic asks you a question like "what type of car you drive?" just give a vague answer like "I drive a white car." Even if she's asking you a question that gives you the opportunity to brag or boast about your accomplishments just give a simple vague answer. This will only make her wonder what type of car you do drive. If it's a nice car she'll be impressed that you didn't try to use that to impress her. That'll let her know that you're good enough as is and don't need accessories to attract women.

## DATING CONVERSATION DO'S AND DON'TS

Dating conversation topics can be one of the trouble areas for men. On one hand you want to have a stimulating conversation but on the other hand you want to remain a mystery. So what's the balance? Always let women do a majority of the talking on dates. When men talk too much you always run the risk of talking yourself out the booty. Women are not logical and there isn't exactly a right or wrong answer to a question, everything just hinges on how she's feeling in the moment. Stay away from politics, religion and sex topics. People treat politics and religion like it's the end all be all. When you're on a date with a woman there's a good chance she's looking for a reason to disqualify you. Some women might find that if your political beliefs or religion is different from hers it could be a deal breaker. Now I know what you're thinking, isn't she going to find out anyway? That's true, but she might be a little more open minded a month into the both of you dating than she would on the first or second date. Try to avoid talking about past relationships. I said try because she might bring it up. If she brings it up always speak highly of your ex. If she asks, "why did you two break up?" Just say "we grew apart" or "we both started finding different interests in life" and leave it at that. Stay away from sex talk, even if she starts it first. Women do this little cat and mouse game and as soon as you engage in this type of conversation she could back up and lose interest. You're much better off sticking to conversations like favorite vacation locations, plans for the future, hobbies and interest etc. You want to let her know you're happy in life and enjoying what you do for a living because women fear getting with a man who hates his life and hoping she can be his source of happiness. Don't discuss your job and passion too long though because you run the risk of trying to sell yourself. You have to learn how to feed the conversation. Feeding the conversation basically means having the ability to ask a woman follow-up questions to keep her talking. The more she talks means the less you're talking. The less you talk the better your chances of not talking yourself out the booty. Basically, just get to know her without any edgy topics. Don't be afraid if there's silence on the date. That's when most guys break frame and turn into a dancing monkey to keep the woman talking. In their minds they're thinking she must be bored, losing interest or has lost interest so let me entertain her so she knows I'm a fun guy to hang out with. That's when most men just start talking about absolutely anything to get the woman back talking. Always hold frame and never get nervous if the woman gets quiet, it could be a test. Non-confident men show their lack of confidence when a woman gets quiet. If you turn into an entertainer, you could find yourself in the friend zone or even worse, the jerk-you-around zone.

## PHYSICAL ESCALATION AND CLOSING THE DEAL

The faster you can raise a woman's interest the faster you can sleep with her. You can't sleep with a woman until her interest reaches at least the 80-90% range. She could have high initial interest and you lower it by making silly mistakes like over pursuing, i.e., double texting, asking to see a woman twice in a week, calling too much. For the sake of getting my point across let's assume you've been following all the strategies I've laid out in this book and you've got her back to your place; you still have to seal the deal. Women are programmed to present themselves as a challenge. She's more than likely not going to come in the house and just strip naked, you're going to have to seal the deal. Whether you know it or not the physical escalation has been going on since you met her. Everything you've done or haven't done since you met her is what has her on your couch now. Patience is the key to closing the deal with women. It's a simple cat and mouse game at this point. With women the testing never stops, even when they're on your couch getting ready to sleep with you. Women are subconsciously always searching for the highest value man they can find. These happen to be men that are already getting laid. Men that are already getting laid don't get impatient or upset. Men who don't get laid get upset, impatient or think the woman doesn't want them sexually because they're inexperienced with women and don't know how to seal the deal. Sealing the deal with women basically boils down to simple seduction progressions. You both are sitting down on the couch and so it's time to make your move. First ask her to move in closer to you. You don't move in closer to her because that's submissive. Instruct her to come closer so she stays in her feminine energy. A woman needs to be in her feminine energy to submit to a man sexually, so it's imperative to keep a woman in her feminine. Once she comes closer wait a couple of minutes and proceed to kiss her on the neck. Some women will stop you, some women will not. If she doesn't stop you proceed to move your hand to her thigh. Most women will stop you after a few seconds. This is a test, she doesn't want you to think she's easy or maybe she just wants to slow things down a bit. In any effect you stop and talk about something else. Don't sit there quiet because it could come off as you're upset and that could get her uncomfortable. It gets her uncomfortable because if she goes any further with you she's not quite sure you can stop if she asks you to. Once a woman gets uncomfortable it could kill her mood to engage in sex. Never give her the idea that you're upset that she stopped you. Bring up a subject and chat about that for a few minutes before you try again. Once you start again you start back with her neck. Always go back to first base which is her neck. Work your way to her thigh again and typically she won't stop you this time. If she hasn't stopped you yet, you want to progress to her chest. I can pretty much guarantee you she'll stop you again. If she does you simply stop and chat for a few minutes before you give it another try. Start back with the neck again and work your way to her thigh. If she doesn't stop you proceed to her chest. If she doesn't stop you again you want to progress down to her vagina area. The whole time you're kissing her on her neck. She'll more than likely stop you again. Rinse and repeat until you're back at the vagina area again. Usually she won't stop you this time if you took your time. Make out with her for a few minutes to get her all hot and ready for sex. At this point you want to invite her to the bedroom. You've done everything right by showing you're high value and now she's ready to submit to you in the bedroom. This has to be said and understood; if you don't have the knowledge or skill to close the deal it's a very good chance you won't get a second chance. Women don't handle rejection well, and you not closing the deal could be perceived as a rejection or you just don't understand women. That don't mean you rape the woman but if it's the 3rd date you need to have the patience and skill to close the deal. If it's the third date or later and the seduction hasn't worked and she's still pushing you away, then it's a good chance you killed the attraction by not making her feel comfortable. It's a good chance she declines your offer for another date If you ask her but if you decide to ask her anyway and she accepts make sure you have better patience and control this time around because this could definitely be your last chance.

## BEING GOOD IN THE BEDROOM

It was once upon a time when you could sleep with women and making her climax was not of utmost importance, but things have changed. Thanks to the sexual revolution and feminism women no longer tolerate men who can't or won't please them in the bedroom. When a woman had sex with you back in the day even if the sex wasn't the best in the world she would be willing to make it work because she had done invested her body. A woman sleeping with you back in the day actually meant something, now it means nothing. A woman will sleep with you on Monday and never call or respond to your calls if you don't please her. If you plan on building a nice rotation of women to sleep with it would be of great importance to improve your bedroom skills. Don't let having a small penis and being a premature ejaculator hinder you from building your rotation. The first thing you need to know about having sex with women is that it's much easier making them climax if they have an emotional attachment to you. So the first thing you have to do is have a woman so emotionally involved with you that the mere sight of you makes her wet. You accomplish this emotional attachment by being focused on your purpose and letting her chase your validation, maintaining a masculine frame and having her submit to you. In my opinion the most important part of sex physically speaking is foreplay. It typically takes women a lot longer to climax than men. Also most women can only climax if they're receiving direct clitoris stimulation. The whole point of this is to get a woman right to the edge of climaxing. That's when you penetrate her and the both of you can cum together. She'll think you are the best lover ever. If you're a premature ejaculator I would definitely prioritize the foreplay. Secondly, I would wear two condoms. Wearing two condoms would kill a lot of the sensation in your penis and prevent you from ejaculating too soon. Another strategy you could use would be to constantly change positions. This would provide you a slight break right when you were on the verge of climaxing. I have three positions I use. That's missionary, doggy style and her on top. I just cycle back and forth in between these positions. A tactic I used back in the day would be to jack off before having sex. I stopped using that tactic because I noticed my erection sometimes wouldn't be as hard as normal. Understand these strategies work for you even if you're not a premature ejaculator. I never heard a woman complain about a man lasting too long in the bedroom. We all could last a little bit longer to be honest. There could come a time when you meet a woman with whom you have an extremely high physical attraction or a woman who has what's commonly referred to as "red snapper." That's a name given to a woman with a tight grip vagina. If you're ever lucky enough to encounter one of these women please believe you're going to need every strategy you can find to keep from premature ejaculating. My biggest issue in my life has come when I encountered a woman I had an extremely high attraction for. I could never last as long with a dime like I could a seven or eight. I lost a couple of very attractive women due to this problem. I made it a priority to improve my sex skills to prevent me from losing high quality women.

## WOMEN DISAPPEARING AFTER SEX

Men have been fed this myth that all women want monogamous relationships. So men are dumbfounded when they sleep with women and never hear from them again. Men instantly think "did I do something wrong?" or "was I bad in bed?" when in actuality there's a lot of women who actually enjoy meaningless sex just as much as men. To be fair sometimes the woman could have not enjoyed the sexual encounter but in most cases I'm willing to bet the woman is probably involved with someone else, on a break from someone else or just enjoys casual sex. Don't take it personal, it comes with the territory. I think more guys are starting to understand this more and more due to female nature being exposed. Men have to rid themselves of this beta male mindset that all women want a husband and something meaningful. This is post sexual revolution, women have been taught that they too can have carefree flings also. Sex used to really mean something to women. It was once upon a time where if a woman had sex with you and had given you her body she had an investment in you. Unfortunately, that day no longer exists and women can have sex with no strings attached just like a man. Men need to have more of an abundant mindset when dealing with women these days.

## HOW TO PURSUE AFTER SEX

You've finally gotten what you've been attempting to get for nearly a month or longer and you're wondering how to proceed afterwards. If all you wanted was sex then fine, never call her again, you don't owe her anything but if its continued sex you're looking for you'll need to know the rules of engagement or you'll be having another hole in your rotation very soon. As fast as you raised a woman's attraction, you can lower it twice as fast. So the first thing you need to know is that the game never ends. Always stay on your purpose. Never make a woman your top priority, that's a turn off even if they're asking for it. I told you women are backwards, they say one thing but respond to another. First things first, always call a woman the next day after sex unless you don't plan on dating her on a consistent basis. If you just want to hang out with her every blue moon then wait a few days or a week even. It don't matter if she's upset or not because you're sending a message to her that you're only interested in casual sex. If she's not cool with that then cool, just consider it a one night stand and move on but if she's cool with it then you now have another woman with booty on standby. If you want to see her on a regular basis then you need to call her the next day. Not doing so could turn her off. That could be a sign of low interest to her or even worse, a rejection. She could also take it as you're not looking for something more serious and if she is she might feel like she's wasting her time dating you. So it basically boils down to what your goals are with her as in how to proceed. If you choose to date her on a consistent basis and she's pursuing you it's ok to pursue her more consistently also as long as she's reciprocating but if she pulls back, you pull back. Never pursue her more than she pursues you. With feminism being the way it is it's unlikely a woman pursues you much if at all until her feelings develop but if she does then it's ok to pursue a bit more. If you're looking to have a fling then be more sporadic as the woman will more than likely never pursue you.

## HOW TO KEEP SLEEPING WITH WOMEN WHO ARE FEELING USED

There will come a time when a woman will want more of your non-sexual attention. Understand this, fellas, the trade supposed to be non-sexual attention for sexual attention unless the woman doesn't find you attractive, then it's a trade of monetary gain i.e., expensive dates, gifts, trips or money for sexual attention. If you have a rotation of women and you're focused on your purpose some of the women, once their feelings develop, will eventually feel they're not getting a fair trade of non-sexual attention for sexual attention. The key here is to listen to the woman. If you want to keep sleeping with this woman you're going to need to give her a little more of your non-sexual attention but there is a balance. If you give her too much of your non-sexual attention she could start to lose attraction because you're not acting high value by being too available. If you keep being distant and don't start giving her more of your non-sexual attention she could lose attraction because she doesn't feel she's getting a fair deal. Let's put it like this, fellas; hypothetically let's say you've taken a woman out three times and she hasn't slept with you yet, you're going to start to feel used. As a wise woman I once dated told me, everybody wants something out of the deal. The secret to keep sleeping with a woman like this is to constantly keep selling how busy your purpose has you. When you're dating women, you should every now and then be talking about how occupied your purpose has you. The key here is every now and then. You don't want to come off as you're selling your earning potential. Don't wait until she asks you to give her more of your non-sexual attention. If you can sell it, a good woman would never try to impede his progress. By the way, this should be true by the way. You really should be busy on your purpose.

## HOW TO KEEP SLEEPING WITH A WOMAN WHO WANTS A RELATIONSHIP

No matter how tight your game is or how smooth you think you are there will come a time when the woman wants to know "where is this going?" You my friend have just been given an ultimatum. To the classic beta male this is music to his ears. This is what he's been wanting since he first got her number but for us guys who are only interested in casual sex with a variety of women this is what we've been dreading. We knew it was only a matter of time. The good news is you've done a good job of raising her interest high enough to where she's asking you this question. The bad news is some women will walk if they don't get the answer they want to hear. The reason women give men this ultimatum is because women know their value is based off their physical appearance primarily. The last thing most women want to do is to waste time with a man who doesn't want more than casual sex. Time is not on a woman's side. Women are losing their sexual market value daily so the more time she wastes waiting on you to decide if you want something more the less likely she is to land a high-value man in the future. If you want to keep sleeping with this woman you need to learn how to dangle the carrot in front of her so to speak. You simply state that you like the way things are progressing, but you don't like to rush into anything. Tell her that if things keep progressing a relationship might be something you're interested in in the future. If she's hell bent on getting an answer right now, then let her go if that's not something you're interested in. If she's willing to wait, string her along as long as you can until she finally realizes that you're not interested in something serious. Don't feel guilty you're leading her on? The whole point of me writing this book is to even out the playing field between men and women. The reason men are so frustrated with women these days is because men were playing with one set of rules while women were playing with another. Women have been stringing men along for the longest time with no regret. You're probably dating a woman right now who knows she's never going to sleep with you but she's going to use you for free dates and attention for as long as she can. We as men have to stop playing by one set of rules while women lie, cheat and manipulate their way to getting whatever they want. Lead her on for as long as you can, if she finally figures out that you only want one thing then let her go and move on. Keep your abundance mindset, never agree to a relationship if that's not what you want to just keep a woman. Men do that every day all around the world just to keep a woman, then wonder why they're miserable later.

## EXPECT TO LOSE WOMEN IN YOUR ROTATION

Guys have to accept the fact that they're going to lose women out of their rotation from time to time. If you're a red pilled guy and are totally against being in a relationship, it's totally illogical to expect women to be content with being nothing more than a glorified sex buddy forever. First let's talk about what it takes to get and keep a woman in your rotation. To get a woman in your rotation it simply means you had enough game and charm to build and maintain a woman's attraction. Not a simple feat by no means. The building is easy for the most part but it's a daunting task to maintain that attraction. The catch is it's only logical that the woman wants more of a commitment over time as her feelings develop. More times than not, when a woman is just one of many women in a man's rotation, the man is giving the woman very minimal non-sexual attention but still gets to sleep with the woman at least once a week. Let's be honest here, this arrangement mainly benefits the man unless he's giving financial support. At some point it's only reasonable for the woman to want more. Every woman's timetable is different depending on attraction level, age and personal beliefs, etc. To gain this commitment most women at some point will ask you flat out "where is this going?" Meaning time to shit or get off the pot, mister. Now I teach men to string it out as long as they can by insinuating that they prefer to take things slow but that will only work so long until the woman tires of waiting for you to make a decision. At some point in the dating phase if the woman still hasn't seen progression in the courtship you can expect her to pullback. A pullback is always a last-ditch effort to get what she wants.

The pullback from a woman in your rotation is different from the pullback of a girlfriend. The girlfriend pullback is to either gain the upper hand in the relationship, she's losing interest or just wants to break the monotony in the relationship. Remember women need chaos in their lives to stay emotionally engaged. Please understand that when a woman who's in your rotation reaches this point it's not about what you have or haven't done as far as over pursuing or under pursuing, it's simply a game of chicken. In other words, who blinks first. If you're a high-value male and truly red pilled, then you will be ready to pass this test. Be warned though, some women aren't testing and will move on. The trade is sexual attention for non-sexual attention. Men wouldn't want to deal with women who they are giving lots of non-sexual attention with no sexual attention, so you can't expect a woman to be content with giving you sexual attention with minimal non-sexual attention forever and a day. Going forward if you're a red pilled man you should expect every woman you date to walk out of your life at some point. Even if you're not red pilled don't expect women to stick around forever while you make up your mind. Women know most men have a pretty good idea if a woman is girlfriend or wifey material for them within 2-3 months. After a woman hits you with the ultimatum, she has a timetable in her head as far as how long she's willing to wait.

## IMPORTANCE OF HOLDING MASCULINE FRAME

One of the biggest detriments when dating or when you are in a relationship with a lady is men aren't able to maintain a masculine frame. A masculine frame is when a man is in a calm, assertive and non-emotional mind frame. This means you are not to ever argue with a woman. Doing so means you're allowing the woman to move you off center. Women are emotional so you're never going to get logic or rationale from them anyway so what's the point in arguing? More times than not women like to start arguments just to break the monotony of the relationship. You have to maintain your composure and confidence. Remain assertive with women. To be assertive with women means that you're a man who doesn't issue idle threats. It simply means that if a woman is displaying behavior not to your liking you simply have no problem moving on to the next woman. It's not about raising your voice and throwing temper tantrums, it's about a woman knowing you mean what you say and say what you mean. Men need to understand that this is your woman and not your homie or best friend. Your woman wants a man not an immature kid. That don't mean you can't joke around with your girl from time to time, but it has to be done in a masculine seductive frame and not a goofy cornball type of way. At the end of the day you can do what you want but don't go crying when your woman has lost respect for you. There are other benefits to maintaining a masculine frame. Everyone you encounter, not just women, will show you respect if you can hold a masculine assertive frame. Holding a masculine frame physiological and physical. This means that your body language is also involved in maintaining a masculine frame. This means an upright posture with shoulders back and head up. Also, be cognizant to make eye contact. When you carry yourself like a masculine man and when you're out with your girl other men naturally give you respect. Any man who has dated a hot chick knows that it can be a challenge at times to get guys or haters to not try to start trouble but holding a masculine frame can definitely help you in this aspect.

## BE PROACTIVE, NOT REACTIVE

I teach guys to be proactive not reactive when dealing with women. That means instead of waiting for her to stir things up, you stir things up. To accomplish this, you simply disappear for an entire day once every 4-6 weeks and she can't reach you. Not if you're living together of course. This means for 24 hours she can't get ahold of you. This forces a woman to engage her emotions, which is needed by the way to maintain attraction. Women gravitate towards the bad boy so to speak because they provide the emotional rollercoaster women need to engage their emotions. You don't have to do drive-bys or robbing banks to get a woman to engage her emotions. All you have to do is don't fall into a routine. Routines are good for men because we are logical and like consistency. Women are the complete opposite. They need things to be spiced up from time to time. This is why things will be moving smoothly in the relationship and out of nowhere she'll start world war 3. Why live on the defensive? Be proactive in your approach and create the turmoil she needs. Provide that turmoil every woman needs from time to time to give them the emotional stimulation they need to maintain attraction.

## HOW TO BUILD AND MAINTAIN YOUR ROTATION

Once you've mastered or at least got the hang of dating, you'll need to understand how to build and maintain a rotation. A rotation of women you're dating is the ultimate skill of every alpha male walking the earth. It takes the right balance of non-sexual attention and strategy to pull it off. The first things you need to learn how to do are balancing a budget and managing a schedule. Dating multiple women can be a very expensive task if not managed properly even if you're keeping the outings cheap. So first thing you have to figure out is how much disposable income you can spend on outings with your women. Stay within your budget. Next thing is learning how to manage a schedule if you're not accustomed to doing so. Most smartphones are equipped with a digital calendar, start booking all your dates in your calendar schedule like a business so you never have any confusion. Make sure all your other women understand that you're dating other women. It's ok to lead women on if they have hopes of getting a relationship out of you but never ever tell a woman she's your girlfriend or she's the only other woman you're dating if you're dating other women. It'll do nothing but cause unnecessary drama. Learn your women's schedules so you know what days work best for each woman. After a while they should know their "day." Make sure they know you're dating other women because women are notorious for leaving articles of clothing over when they leave your place. This is called nesting. They do that intentionally so other women whom you may have over can discover them. It's all a ploy to have you to themselves. The thing is if you're being honest with the women you're dating there should be no problem if they do discover them. In fact, if you've been honest it'll probably help you in the fact that she now knows other women find you sexually appealing.

## USING ONLINE DATING TO BUILD YOUR ROSTER

One of the best tools to build your rotation is online dating. Although I still prefer men to meet women in person, it's still a good tool to use. The reason I prefer men to meet women in public is because we as men can attract women with more than just physical appearance. Women unfortunately have to primarily rely solely on their appearance because men are mostly visual. When you use online dating as your primary or sole tool to meet women you don't get to show your charm, humor, confidence, etc. If you're short or overweight you're really doing yourself a disservice by relying on online dating. When you're leaving it up to a profile pic or a profile of course the woman is going to make her decision by physical appearance. Now that I've gotten all the drawbacks out the way, I'll tell you the strategy I use to have sex with dozens of women online. First things first; remember guys, you're always displaying high-value characteristics no matter if you're online or in the real world. You want to send one message a day online to a woman unless she's displaying high interest. You can judge a woman's interest online by the kind of responses she gives you. For example, you send her a message saying, "good morning I'm jessie, what's your name?" She responds with "Joanne." You then proceed to ask her "what's your favorite thing to do in your spare time?" She replies with "swimming." Those my friend are what we call low interest responses or a woman whose only online looking for attention. When a woman has high interest she'll write you a decent size response. She won't send one-word responses like the before mentioned. Another thing you'll notice is that she asks you questions. Notice any similarities to meeting women in public? If you approach women in public and they're genuinely interested, they'll give you the same kind of responses. Same rules apply for if they're not interested in person, also, they'll give you all these one-word responses. Always pay attention to a woman's attraction level whether you're online or in person, doing so will keep you from wasting a lot of time and energy. If you recognize a woman has high interest, you're going to pursue her differently. You want to respond to her message within a few hours instead of the next day. Women lose interest in men who don't respond to the fact they're displaying high interest. She'll just accept your very slow responses as low interest or rejection. When women display low interest, you want to respond to the message the following day to show that you're high-value male and that you have a life. In doing so you'll hopefully raise her interest because you're displaying high-value male characteristics. These are the traits that preselected men display. It'll take a little longer to raise her interest because physically you're not her ideal match but remember what I said about us men having other attributes to raise women's sex interest level but at least you have your foot in the door. When I'm sending the questions it's always the same questions. "Good afternoon I'm jessie, what's your name?" "What's your favorite thing to do in your spare time?" "How often do you come to the city?" "What's your favorite spot in the city?" and lastly "We should get a drink, when are you usually free?" Once she sends that I say, "ok cool, send me your number so we can set up a time to meet." I then send her my number, it's that simple. I then use my normal way of pursuit once I've gotten her number.

## HOW TO ORGANIZE YOUR ROTATION

Finding time to date multiple women simultaneously can be costly financially and time wise. When I'm organizing my rotation, I organize my women in four groups. Women I'm sleeping with who have high interest, women in the friend zone, prospects with high interest and prospects with low interest. Now I preach for men to be on their purpose so let's presuppose you are saving the dating for the weekend. We know how flaky and unpredictable women are. One day they're all over you in love and the next day they're pulling back wanting space. It's important for men to always be grooming prospects. Women do this to a science. They'll string along your replacement for months and sometimes years if the man allows it. Women seem to understand this but most men date one woman at a time and wonder why they act so needy. The proper way to organize your roster to always have the women you're sleeping with to be in the last position. In other words, date your prospects before you meet up with the women you're sleeping with. For instance, I typically would meet up with a high or low interest prospect around 6 or 7 pm. Have a drink or two and then meet up with the woman I'm sleeping with. Doing this will also keep you in an abundance mindset and help you pass your prospects' shit test. If you're pressed for time and can only date a couple women don't worry about trying to date the low interest prospects. Only date low interest prospects if you don't have high interest prospects. If you don't have any women you're sleeping with then date the low interest prospects before you go on a date with a high interest prospect. In other words, you would meet a low interest prospect around 7 pm and meet up with a high interest prospect around 9 pm. The reason you do this is because you probably can sleep with the high interest prospects if you do nothing to lower her interest over the date.

## Maintaining a Woman's Interest

You've mastered attracting women and sleeping with them. Let's be honest, there's going to be a large portion of women you sleep with that you never want to see again. On the other hand, there's going to be a small portion that you want to keep dating. The problem with most men is getting too comfortable. When a man finds a woman he truly likes he starts focusing more on her and less on his purpose and passion. At first the woman might enjoy and appreciate all this attention but after a while she gets bored with you. Basically, she starts taking you for granted because you're giving her your time without her having to work for it. Women treat your time and attention just like anyone else treats anything that comes too easy, like it's worthless. To keep women interested in you, always make them work for your time, that way they always appreciate you. Another benefit of staying on your purpose in case you needed another reason is that women love ambitious men. When a woman sees a man building an empire she wants to remain on her best behavior so she can make it to the finish line. Women love growth. It doesn't matter if you're making six figures currently, women remain attracted to men who are striving for more growth. Validation is like kryptonite to women. You want women constantly chasing your validation, not just giving it to them. Women not only want a man who can stand up to them in the beginning stages but also the dating or relationship stage. When men start getting emotionally attached they start letting women get away with disrespect. Women see this as weakness and start losing attraction. The game never ends, whether it's the first date or you've been married for fifty years, you have to always remain masculine enough to pass women's tests. If a woman sees this kind of weakness she'll start testing to see what else she can get away with. One way women like to test men they're dating on a consistent basis is to test your insecurities. She might flirt with another guy in front of you to see how you react. If you say anything, you've failed this test. Act as if you don't see anything. Another way she might test you is to not answer her phone around you even though it's just her mom or sister. A woman can just throw these jealousy tests at you and she can find out a whole lot about your confidence. As a man you're supposed to feel there's no way another man has the ability to take your woman. The longer you know a woman the more attached you're going to be and the harder it's going to be to pass these tests. That's why staying on your purpose is key to passing these tests. When you're truly invested in seeing your purpose and passion come to fruition, you're too busy to get too attached to a woman which is going to keep her interest high. She'll be too busy competing for time against your purpose instead of shit testing you. Women hate emotional weakness. I can't think of a faster way to lower a woman's attraction. Never argue with women. You'll never get logic anyway, you'll only get emotion. Also arguing with women puts them in their masculine energy since you're moving into your feminine energy. When conversing with women always remain in a masculine calm demeanor. If you remain in a masculine frame, she'll remain in a feminine frame. Women lose attraction to a man who's in his feminine energy. Women are emotionally unstable, if a man is as emotional as she is who's supposed to make her feel safe when things get tough? Women need security from men, not just financial security but mental security. Women need the security of knowing a man is masculine enough to handle any situation if anything so happens to arise.

## GETTING A WOMAN TO CRAVE YOU SEXUALLY

I've touched on this earlier, but I would like to get a little deeper on this subject. It's that important. This can be the reason you have ten women craving you sexually or you have a lot of one-night stands, none of which are your choice by the way. Sex is very critical these days to building and maintaining a rotation. A wise man once said "she always comes because I always make her cum!" There's a lot of truth to that little saying. If you want a woman to stay in your rotation you are going to have to learn how to make her cum. Now contrary to what you might think the best way to get a woman to cum is mentally. When you hold a masculine frame and a woman has complete respect for you there's not much you can do wrong inside the bedroom. When you have that much mind control over a woman just you touching her sends an electric current through her body. When you have a woman's head this much it don't matter if physically you're not her best lover, every stroke you give her has an emotional attachment to it. Your five inches will feel like ten. So getting in a woman's mind should be your first option. If you get her mind, the body follows. Let's be honest here, sometimes you won't be able to get a woman emotionally wrapped in you. This is where improving your foreplay and sex game comes into play. Speaking for myself, foreplay changed my sex life. I used to overlook it, but I quickly realized its importance. Once I started foreplay I noticed a high return of women. It's very hard for a woman to cum without direct clitoris stimulation. You should be kissing a woman on her lips, neck or chest while you're playing with her clitoris with your fingers. Do this for about ten mins or until she starts convulsing like she's about to cum, then stick your penis in so your penis gets the credit. She'll think you have the magic stick. That should do the trick but if it doesn't there's still one last thing you can try. After you've done the foreplay you could try letting her get on top to finish the job. When you let her get on top you're letting her find her own spot. Women know their body much better than you'll ever know it. Letting her get on top allows her to contour her body to hit her g-spot. Most times you'll see a woman on top lean back, that's because she's trying to get your penis to rub up against her clitoris. Under no circumstances are you to perform oral sex. It's too submissive and validating. You'll lower her attraction if you do. I'm not saying you'll never see her again and I'm not saying she won't enjoy it but what I am saying is she might start shit testing you since you're essentially submitting to her. Women love oral sex just like they love compliments but if you do either they tend to lose a little attraction and the shit testing begins. Performing oral sex on a woman is the most validating thing you could do. Remember once you give a woman your validation she starts making you chase hers.

## THE SILENT TREATMENT AND SEXLESS RELATIONSHIP

There's been a misunderstanding of two aspects in a relationship between men and women. That misunderstanding is that women stop talking or having sex with their mate to manipulate them. While that may be true in some cases by and large women do this because their interest is at an all-time low. When a woman's attraction gets too low she simply doesn't care enough to argue, hence the silent treatment. Essentially what the woman is saying in a situation like this is my attraction is so low I don't care to even argue with you right now. If a woman stops sleeping with you then it simply means your feminine behavior has her to the point where she can't even submit to you. That's right guys, when a woman opens her legs to you she is being submissive to you. Arguing with women, acting needy etc. are all feminine traits. When in this situation a man should never ask a woman what's wrong or anything like that. No need in trying to get logic from an irrational creature. You would get a lot further with her by simply refocusing on your purpose and making her start to chase your validation again. When a man loses focus on his purpose in life and makes a woman the primary focus in his life a woman will lose attraction. Now there's levels to low attraction. You have the low attraction where the woman is shit testing you a lot and if you keep failing these shit tests you find yourself in the hopeless position of the silent treatment. Focusing on your purpose fixes this because when a man knows he's headed somewhere, he has the ability to constantly pass women's shit tests therefore foregoing the dreaded silent treatment. Women subconsciously test constantly. A man who's unsure of himself is incapable of constantly passing these tests. He starts to wonder if some other guy who makes more money than him is hitting on his woman when he's not around. This insecurity lowers the woman's attraction. He then proceeds to want to spend more time with her in the hopes of preventing another man the opportunity to take her away. An insecure man is not a confident man. We all know confidence is the biggest attraction for females. A man on his purpose is a confident man. Confident men don't get the silent treatment and they definitely don't have sexless relationships. When a woman is chasing your validation, she's being submissive. So she is naturally turned on by you sexually due to your masculine dominant state.

## THE PULLBACK

One of the biggest mysteries since the beginning of time has been men trying to figure out what a woman wants. To be honest I'm not quite sure women know what they want but I'll give it a shot. Feminine women want a man that remains confident and assertive even when he cares deeply about them. Feminine women want a man who knows how to lead. Never ask a feminine woman where she wants to go for dinner. Always be in control, feminine women hate leading. They just want to show up and look pretty and not have to lead a man. It goes with their feminine nature to follow a masculine man. If you display any of those feminine traits with a feminine woman she'll always pullback. When women lose interest they pull back, that is when they become withdrawn and a little distant from their man. Things you'll see when your woman pulls back are less intimacy; she'll spend less time with you, she won't initiate contact as much if at all and she'll seem colder and distant. When a woman pulls back it means she has one foot out the door. It means that if you don't turn things around quick you'll lose her. Women also use the pullback to get the power in the relationship. The power is whoever leads the relationship. When a woman pulls back most men become weak and submissive to make her happy. This is mainly done by masculine women who want to lead the relationship. Feminine women tend to pullback when a man is more into his feminine energy than the woman causing her to lose attraction. In order to turn things around you need to really spend more time on your purpose. She's gotten a little too familiar and comfortable with you. The only way to counter a woman's pullback is to pull back yourself. That'll raise her interest because absence makes the heart grow fonder. That's only half the battle though. Now that she's begging for your time it's time to show her you're a leader and masculine. Since you've gotten refocused on your purpose that little bit of swagger you lost has come back. Now you don't fail her little shit test anymore. A man has to be always focused on his purpose. It keeps him busy and confident. Don't look at the pullback as a bad thing, look at it as a warning sign. A warning sign that should be taken seriously if you want to keep your woman. Look at it as an opportunity to regain focus on your purpose and regain control of your relationship.

## THE BREAKUP

Let's presuppose you didn't take heed to your woman's pullback and continued your beta male behavior; you are probably broken up trying to figure out where you went wrong. Well like I mentioned earlier, if you don't take immediate action once a woman pulls back you are going to have a few lonely nights ahead unless you have a couple of other women on the side. The only course of action to take now if you have let it get this far is to go no contact. No contact lets a woman know you're not crying and pining over her and that you have the ability to move on. Showing a woman that you have the ability to move on lets her know that you have other options or that you have the confidence to meet other women. The reason you're even in this predicament is because you show low value towards the end of the relationship, going no contact lets her know that you're emotionally strong and confident. Men who are mentally weak and lacking confidence will try pleading with the woman to give him another chance, but this only lowers her attraction even more. If you don't remember nothing else I say remember this: begging or pleading with a woman to get back together kills any chance of getting her back. Men have this strange notion that if they show a woman how much they're hurting or miss her that women will take pity on them and get back together with them once they see how much pain they're in. Men need to understand one thing about women, they're only concerned with their feelings. If she has other interest or no interest in you any longer it won't matter how much pain you're in, she could care less if she no longer has feelings towards you. Going no contact is no immediate fix or even a guarantee to work at all. It could be a possibility that she stayed with you long after any attraction was left. If that's the case it's a possibility that no contact or anything else you try could raise her interest back up to a level where she's sleeping with you again. In any case you're never supposed to wait around for a woman to decide if she wants to get back with you or even go on an initial date. Always carry on with your life and never wait for a woman to decide what she wants to do with you. High-value men make women fit into their lives, not the other way around. If your woman has broken up with you look at it as an opportunity to get refocused on your purpose and passion. Also look into finding yourself again. When men get into a relationship they start doing more of what the women want to do and less of what they want to do. Get back to doing the things you love and enjoy. Reconnect with friends who you might've not kicked it with as much since your girl didn't approve of them. Women push most guys' friends away in a relationship. A little divide and conquer so to speak. This goes back to the old saying women don't know what they want. On one hand she's pushing your friends away and on the other hand she's complaining that you're crowding her and not giving her space. Always follow the rules in this book and never listen to what women say they want because quite frankly I don't think they really know.

## REGAINING ATTRACTION AFTER A BREAK-UP OR SEPARATION

Regaining attraction from a woman can be a daunting task. Women typically stick around in a relationship long enough to all their feelings are gone to the point that they basically have no love for you anymore. Some women even go as far as having your replacement already in place once they've decided to drop you for good. By this point she's probably already been sleeping with him and developed feelings for him. In a situation like this the only way you'll have a chance to get her back is if the new guy starts making mistakes and you've gone no contact. If he starts screwing up, which will typically be the same way you were screwing up, he'll push her right back into your arms. Here's the rub though, if you found out she had a replacement already in place when she left you why would you want her back? She's already shown you that she's untrustworthy. In a situation like this, if she did reach out and wanted to get back with you simply let her know you didn't like how she ended things and how she's willing to make it up to you. Never just take a woman back after she just bails on you. She needs to understand you're a high-value male and she just can't come in and out of your life like you don't have other options. Afterwards I would not trust her again. I would put her into my friend zone. The man's friend zone is when you use a woman for her sexual attention with very little to no non-sexual attention. I would not take this woman back as a possible girlfriend, she's untrustworthy. Let's suppose she didn't have a replacement lined up after the breakup and she's reached out to see how you're doing, what you say on that initial call could determine if you have a chance to get her back. Understand she's looking for any sign of neediness or desperation. If she gets a hint of neediness or desperation she'll recognize that little if anything about you has changed and end the call with a "well, it was nice hearing from you, good bye." In a situation like this just relax and ask her would she be open to getting drinks. Women will reach out and put themselves in your orbit but it's up to the man to make the date. If she declines, which is unlikely if you didn't come on too strong, never ask her out again. She's probably reaching out to test for a landing spot if her current fling fizzles out or her attraction simply isn't there anymore for you. Only men who aren't focused on their purpose and passion would even care. A man who's focused on his purpose and passion knows that it's just a matter of time before he can attract any woman he wants. There's an old saying that goes a little like this: you lose money chasing women, but you never lose women chasing paper. Let's assume she accepted your invitation for drinks. Understand that she's going to probably test the hell out of you since you showed insecurities and weakness in the past. You should be a changed man by now. A lot stronger mentally than you were before. If you can pass her test her attraction for you will grow and the both of you can get back together. Always move at the woman's pace. Rushing her back into a relationship will only make you look needy again. Let her do most of the pursuing since she'll be checking for neediness. Show her that you're no longer that weak man with insecurities and you'll hear these magic words once again soon: "I love you!"

## MEN'S FRIENDZONE

In case you missed the memo, women are notorious for using men for their non-sexual attention by relegating men to the friend zone. Well, the tables have changed, men now can put women in the friend zone. Putting a woman in the friend zone simply means you have removed all of your non-sexual attention and she is simply a glorified sex buddy at this point. When you're dating a woman or in a relationship sometimes women can get too comfortable and you checking her does little to stop her bad masculine non-submissive behavior. In a situation like this I advocate the man demoting the woman to the friend zone. The reason I advocate men putting women in the friend zone opposed to completely leaving the woman alone is because you never know when a drought is looming. Us men can't replace women as fast as women can replace us. If I was you I would keep that woman as a spare tire. It doesn't matter how annoying she is, you're basically just having sex with her at this point. It shouldn't be that hard to tolerate her for a few minutes until you cum. You can make up any excuse as to why you're too busy to spend some of your non-sexual attention with her. You can say you're working a lot, working on your purpose, it really doesn't matter what excuse you use. Don't worry about the woman's feelings because it's her bad behavior which has landed her in the friend zone. If she has genuine interest you might see her behavior change. If she's pursuing you really hard take advantage of the situation and maybe ask her for a threesome. See the fact of the matter is you removing your non-sexual attention has her in a scarcity mind state with you. She fears losing you altogether so she's willing to do whatever it takes to keep from losing you. In my experience a woman like this never fully changes. If you take her back fully it's a good chance she eventually ends up acting the same way as before. I would keep her in competition mode. Keep her chasing that carrot but never give it to her.

## MANIPULATOR OR MANIPULATED

It's no secret why women dress sexy, wear make-up, heels, hair weave, etc. They're trying to make themselves as beautiful as possible to attract the highest quality mate they can and to manipulate the beta males into doing everything under the sun to appease them. Women have been manipulating men since the beginning of time. I don't know what your religion is but my religion, Christianity, teaches of a woman named Eve manipulating her mate Adam to eat an apple in the garden of Eden. I don't recommend men crying about female manipulation. I recommend men doing a little manipulation themselves. I recommend men getting their financial situation and physical presentation in the best possible position they can to attract the highest quality female they can. Most men know that women love financial security. Instead of whining about female hypergamy, men should be using it to their advantage. The same way women use our lust against us, we should be using their greed against them. Men should be pursuing their dreams and let the women pursue us. If you spend all your time chasing women you're simply chasing your tail. You would be a lot more successful with women if you took that same energy and chased your passion. When a man has his life in order he manipulates women because she's seeing financial security. You don't have to do much because her greed will make her think that she has the magic vagina to lure you into marriage or a relationship. This is what women do to beta males; they lure into giving them all of their non-sexual attention. They show them a little thigh or cleavage and the beta male is sucking up to them for years waiting on their chance to swoop in. They're being manipulated and used. They're going about it all wrong. They would accomplish their goal much better if they spent that time improving their SMV. As the old saying goes, you lose money chasing women, but you never lose women chasing money.

## WHEN IT'S TIME TO MOVE ON

The old saying goes, women don't know what they want. Well there's one thing clear to me, when women start disrespecting their man to a level that is beyond a test she's literally begging the man to break up with her. Women sometimes prefer for safety reasons to push a man away rather than break up with the man. Unfortunately, most men have a scarcity mindset and just tolerate the bitchiness hoping things turn around. This only kills the little attraction and respect she has left for him, unfortunately. Men need to understand one thing about women. THEY DO EVERYTHING FOR A REASON. If she's testing you it's because you're showing weakness. If a woman is being flat out disrespectful it means that you've shown weakness for a very long time and she's lost all respect for you. A woman talking about how attractive other men are right in front of you is not an insecurity test, that's just flat out disrespectful. A woman asking you "can she go to lunch with an ex?" is flat out disrespectful. Now in these situations I'm not referring to women you're just dating. This is relegated to men in monogamous relationships. The whole point of dating as opposed to being in a relationship is simply the fact that no one owes anyone an explanation for anything but if you're in a relationship the whole point of being in a relationship means you're not free to just do whatever you want any more out of respect to your partner. Men have to learn how to be alone and value themselves. There's no way any man can convince me being with a rude bitchy woman is better than being alone. A rude bitchy woman will drive a man crazy. He'll literally hate to come home. If you're wondering when it is a good time to leave the relationship because your woman is acting unruly just understand she's more than likely left the relationship a long time ago. Now I understand kids and assets might be at stake but ask yourself this, do you want your kids seeing a dysfunctional relationship? It'll only make them think that this is the norm. They'll grow up in unhappy relationships thinking that it is ok to be unhappy and miserable. I can't speak for anyone else but there's not an asset on this earth that is worth my piece of mind. No car, no money or home should be worth you remaining with an unruly woman. This simply boils down to having respect for yourself. I can give you all the strategies and games to dating women but it's up to you to have self-respect for yourself. You either are going to be a self-respecting man and move on or keep tolerating women's BS. The choice is yours.

## CHEATING

To me there's nothing that displays a man's insecurities more than a man who cheats on his wife or girlfriend. Now I think most of you reading this book should know by now that I'm not speaking on some moral high ground here. I'm talking about peace of mind. Men who cheat on women are men who gave women a commitment in the hopes of having guaranteed sex because they have a scarcity mindset although they know they don't want to be with one woman all their life. If you know in your heart that you're not ready to be with one woman for the rest of your life, why would you want the headache of constantly looking over your shoulder? If you've gotten this far in this book then you should know by now to always keep a couple of women in your friend zone. That should alleviate any fear of going in the dreaded drought. Also, by staying on your purpose that'll help you keep an abundance mindset and your options plentiful. A man on his purpose and mission in life will never have to worry about going through a drought. If you got into a relationship due to an ultimatum, then that is your fault. When a woman hits you with the ultimatum you simply tell her you're not ready for that right now. If she leaves, she leaves, that's what having an abundance mindset is all about.

## WHAT'S THE END GAME?

Dating multiple women can get tiring and taxing after a while. You start to feel to yourself what's the point of it all? I think every man would love the picture we see on TV of the husband happily married to a submissive wife and two beautiful children. In reality though the wife is a bitch on wheels using the husband as a survival tool. If you're a man and haven't taken the red pill this lifestyle will seem silly to you because you'll be thinking "why don't this guy just grow up?" On the other hand, if you've

seen female nature at its worst then you're fully aware why some men live this lifestyle. Putting it blatantly if you're red pilled then you don't have much respect for female nature. Most red pilled men like myself are prepared and content with dating multiple women to remain detached to women. If you're red pilled then you might at times find yourself wishing you weren't red pill so you could just go back to being a naive beta male simply in love with a woman who only sees you as a survival tool. If you're red pilled, then it's very unlikely you'll ever find love because the mere fact that you're fully knowledgeable of female nature it's impossible to love because a main component of love is trust and it's virtually impossible to love a woman once you're aware of what they are capable of. The end game for most of us red pilled brothers is to just pursue our purpose and make our lives the best that we can. Women will just be icing on the cake. If you haven't mastered the art of being alone then you're never going to be a happy red pilled man. You must learn to be content with yourself first. Women are always going to come and go; when everything is set and done the only thing that'll always be there for you is your purpose in life.

Printed by Amazon Italia Logistica S.r.l.
Torrazza Piemonte (TO), Italy

10032862R00085